T0171594

Sustainable Development Handbook

-

A South Asian Perspective

Aliar Hossain

authorHOUSE®

AuthorHouse™
1663 Liberty Drive
Bloomington, IN 47403
www.authorhouse.com
Phone: 1-800-839-8640

© *2011 Aliar Hossain. All rights reserved.*

No part of this book may be reproduced, stored in a retrieval system, or transmitted by any means without the written permission of the author.

First published by AuthorHouse   1/14/2011

ISBN: 978-1-4567-7197-3 (sc)

Printed in the United States of America

Any people depicted in stock imagery provided by Thinkstock are models, and such images are being used for illustrative purposes only. Certain stock imagery © Thinkstock.

This book is printed on acid-free paper.

Because of the dynamic nature of the Internet, any Web addresses or links contained in this book may have changed since publication and may no longer be valid. The views expressed in this work are solely those of the author and do not necessarily reflect the views of the publisher, and the publisher hereby disclaims any responsibility for them.

Contents

Table of Figures

Dedication

**This book is dedicated to the
loving memory of my father.**

Foreword

Lars Hallen

Sustainable Development is a critical global issue, calling for a new development paradigm involving sustainable development at all levels of education and planning. Population increase, over-consumption, global temperature rise due to increasing emissions of greenhouse gases, rising sea water levels, environmental refugees etc. are actual threats meeting the next generation. South Asia is the most vulnerable area to e.g. rising sea levels and destruction of marine eco systems, and extreme weather conditions followed by flooding has recently caused severe damage to millions of people and their livelihoods in a number of South Asia countries. Against this background this Sustainable Development Handbook with its South Asian perspective is a most valuable and important hands-on contribution to existing learning material about Sustainable Development.

More than 50% of the planets population is under 30 years of age and almost 30% is under 15 years. Thus, education about sustainable development with focus on young people is especially important. Besides, this group is probably the most receptive, if not yet motivated, to learn about sustainable development. I am therefore happy to see that this book has a number of special features which makes it particularly interesting for young people; the historical background (from Earth Day until today), a background analysis covering ethical aspects and poverty issues as important parts of sustainable development, concrete examples from various South Asian countries, a description of a number of various ecosystems, and an overview of sustainable energy to be developed and used in the near future.

Public awareness is probably one of the most important roads leading to the necessary change of attitude required to achieve a sustainable development. I therefore welcome this book as a key contribution to a global sustainable development in the 21st century.

Lars Hallén
Chairman, LIFE Academy
Sweden

Dr. Brendan D'Cruz, Head of Business & Computing, University of Wales, Newport.

I have no doubt about the need for joint international action when it comes to sustainable development. Yet Copenhagen failed. There has been increased skepticism about climate change. People are more focused on economic rather than environmental crises. But sustainable development still matters. All the major indicators such as sea levels, air pollution, glacial melt, snow cover, rising temperatures, declining energy and food sources, deforestation, floods and droughts etc. suggest the world is facing big problems at a time when doing nothing is no longer an option. The developed world is now doing something, but the developing world has to play its part so as to not make the same mistakes to ensure that all our futures are better. We live on the same planet, all of us. So we need actions not avoidance, progress based on good practice, and real results beyond the rhetoric.This book (by Aliar) is one of the first to look specifically at countries in the developing world, and the contribution they should make towards delivering effective global citizenship.

Derek Hall (MBE, Senior Consultant for Environment & Quality Management, Blackmores)

It gives me great pleasure in writing this introduction. I have a great appreciation of Aliar Hossain's efforts to give the reader of this handbook an in-depth background to the complexities of life within South Asia; as well as the wider planetary issues that have an impact on this part of the Asian continent. A key factor also recognized within this handbook is that it is not just the importance of the South Asian Perspective, but also the human perspective.

The author explains that, local communities and global populations have a genuine claim in the actions of business, and that the business leader is but one part of the wider complex machinery of trade and production. This is true, even though not always realized by businesses that work within the restrictions of the current economic system; which tends to isolate the social and environmental requirements into departmental functions. I believe that it is of utmost importance to step beyond this mind set and take a more holistic approach.

I can draw heavily on my experiences at Bovince Limited who operated within the print manufacturing sector. Within this company we developed a variety of interconnecting sustainable work practices, which recognized internal needs and the impacts of various externalities. These requirements were embodied within a structured business model, which was creative, flexible and balanced in approach.

Similarly, identified within this handbook, is the importance of keeping balance; between economic growth, social development and a respect for nature. (See also Figure 1: Global Sustainability Framework). This need for balance is especially important when working through the complex process of integrating the philosophy of sustainability into every day social and business actions. This complexity is recognized by author throughout the handbook. For example, this is shown when interviewing students and citizens from Bangladesh, India, Pakistan and Sri Lanka with regard to seasonal impacts in rural areas; which are susceptible to variations in weather patterns and changes in environmental processes.(See Figure 13: Traditional Six Seasons of South Asia).

The author also states that 'No one country is alike'. And also makes the point that it depends on various components such as country characteristics, technological development, geographical structure, the creativity of the people, etc. Of course the reliance on people within the production processes is of absolute importance. However, what values do us humans put on nature within our daily activities?

We need to learn from the past deeds, to gain an understanding on how to face future circumstances. In the words of Albert Einstein: *'Look! Look! Look deep into nature and you will understand everything'*. To gain a greater understanding of the need for 'Sustainable Development' in South Asia, please continue reading this thought provoking handbook.

Dr Eric CK Chan, Programme Director MA Global Management, Regent's College London-Regents Business School, UK and Human Network Advisor for Life International Foundation for Ecology, Sweden

There is a cry for more efforts and collaborative efforts to raise awareness and implementation to save our planet - Earth, from all kinds of people, organisations and governments. Yet not many have answered the SOS call of the planet. As days goes by the natural resources continue to be drained worldwide. The sudden surge of natural disaster which we are all experiencing came through the effects of global warming. There is a need for all of us to be challenge into a position where we have to stretch outside our comfort zone, then we are forced to expand your consciousness and respond accordingly to this planet emergency. When we are challenged, change is inevitable. The survival of Earth depends on all our continued efforts across country boundaries/cultures and ultimate responsible actions/decisions. Aliar provided some insights/perspectives on the cycle of sustainable change in capacity building for communities from developing nations. The how of processes and frameworks shared could be additional 'keys' to make a difference and unlocked our minds to take responsibility, ownership and spurs us all to move forward and contribute to global sustainable development.

Jonathan A. J. Wilson, Consultant, Senior Lecturer, Researcher, University of Greenwich, London, UK

Sustainable Development is a topic that Aliar Hossain has sought to raise up the agenda, in boardroom discussions. In an impassioned way, he has devoted his time towards highlighting the necessity for such approach – and more particularly in Southeast Asia. The interdependent variables in this region, one could argue makes analysis both more complicated and most definitely crucial to a business' long-term survival. For these reasons, academic literature has seen a flood of dedicated publications that offer a top-down/bottom-up approach specific to each region. However, Sustainable Development is in need of further work, in text and in practice - and to this end, Aliar's book plays it's part. In order to master a region which holds *tigers* and *dragons*, the business world needs a varied toolkit, I am sure that it is Aliar's intention - that the contents of this book will present to readers new ideas and a way forward.

Acknowledgements

My specials thank goes to Lars Hallen (Chairman, Life Academy) for his foreword and for offering his specialist knowledge and expertise in reviewing this handbook.

I would like to thank my friend Danny Winkler for supporting me during the review period and for sharing his experiences in the Maldives. I am grateful to my colleagues Dr. Eric Chan, Dr Brendon D'Cruz, John Wilson and Derek Hall for their comments, advice and motivation. Their thoughts and suggestions have helped to improve the work of a new author. I am also thankful to my students, especially Priyanka Taunk for her assistance while undertaking primary and secondary research. And of course, my gratitude and sincere thanks go to the many individuals who kindly offered their time, opinions and local knowledge to be interviewed during the different field trips spent collecting primary data.

There are many family members and friends to whom I am grateful for their support and motivation, none more so than to my wife for her continuing support, sacrifice and understanding. Finally, I am thankful to my mother who always advised me to think carefully about nature and my actions within it.

Introduction

Today's companies and business leaders can no longer hide from their responsibilities to wider stakeholder communities with claims of ignorance regarding corporate malpractice and failure. At present, the websites and press releases of multinational companies highlight only their positive activities and contributions, without the counter balance of announcements and discussions addressing issues of concern. Given the importance of corporate image in the marketplace, rarely will there be open forums amongst stakeholders to give an informed and complete picture behind the screen or of comparative standards of corporate responsibility in different geographical locations.

Key people and stakeholders are responsible for both the successes and failures of their enterprises, as well as for their own conduct and behaviour. Over the course of the last decades - driven by democratic reforms, increasing social awareness and more integrated global communications networks - the actions of business have increasingly become a concern not just for shareholders but also for the wider community at large. As scientific recognition has affirmed the interdependence of all aspects of planetary functions, local communities and global populations have also established a genuine claim as stakeholders in the actions of business, in which the business leader is but one part of the wider complex machinery of trade and production.

Given this recognition, business ought no longer to be just about running the company as competently as possible in narrow cost and profit terms. Business must address its wider responsibilities, which in economic theory are termed externalities. As is plain to any economist, these externalities form an integral part of the production equation. They cannot be simply brushed under the carpet.

Key people and directors need to travel beyond narrow and traditional corporate governance concerns that simply deal with their well-designed job titles, their salaries, progression strategies, and legal requirements. They must understand how their personal ideals, behaviours, and measures affect the organisations and employees they lead, and also how these shape the surrounding communities within which they are embedded. It requires that one does not divorce personal responsibility from corporate responsibility.

This is the attitude we must adopt if we are to tackle the most pressing issue facing humanity today: the sustainability and evolution of human life, to ensure a satisfactory level of production with which to support human life that is not at the expense of a satisfactory standard of living.

> Human-induced global warming is perhaps the most serious threat that the whole of humanity has ever faced. It is the result of the most profound failure of perception and reason in the history of humanity. Climate change is not really new. Since time began we have had to adapt to changing climatic conditions. However, most of the adjustments humans have made in the past were in response to short-term regionalized climate variations caused by natural events, such as volcanic eruptions and fluctuations in solar radiation. Today, for the first time in history, climate change threatens the entire world and humans are the dominant cause.
>
> (Bob Doppelt)[1]

The tsunami disaster in the Indian Ocean underlines the importance of the global ecosystem and of our fundamental ability to live safely on Planet Earth. In 2004 Sir David King, Chief Scientific Adviser to the UK government, came under attack in the United States of America after voicing his opinion that global warming posed a greater threat than terrorists. Yet his was a positive statement, asserting that it remains within our power to control.

What is happening in the Indian Ocean underlines the

importance of the earth's system to our ability to live safely. And what we are talking about in terms of climate change is something that is really driven by our own use of fossil fuels, so this is something we can manage."[2]

A concerted effort and unbending will are required if we are not to shirk our responsibilties. At the same time, as stakeholders, we are in the best position to progress towards sustainable development. Each era has a challenge, and this is ours. We do it not only to prevent harm, but to build a better and stronger world.

Target Audiences and Why

A growing number of books are available addressing sustainable development and corporate social responsibility, projecting theories and practices, and insightful analysis supported by real-world scenarios and case studies. The main purpose of this handbook is to help individuals, governments, business people and policy makers understand the primary concepts of sustainable development, in order to benefit future generations and support the practice of environmentally sensitive activities.

The author has attempted to create a lucid picture of how changes in the mindset of key political leaders, business leaders and conscious citizens towards a disciplined approach to sustainable development can create a social environment characterised by greater harmony and peace.

There are two target audiences for the Sustainable Development Handbook. The first are mainstream political leaders, business owners, and academics, for whom this book may provide an image of a future in which business success, social and political development, and environmental sustainability are complementary and mutually indispensable achievements. The second audience are the young people who need to be educated about past and present developments in order for them to shape appropriate and better practices in future. This handbook will support the understanding of the concepts of global sustainability and global citizenship.

This handbook is conceived to be accessible to the general public, key policy makers, political leaders and business people in South Asia. Audiences from other developing nations can use it to sample and compare their situations.

The author would also like to suggest the following list as further reading:

- Doppelt, B., *The Power of Sustainable Thinking: How to Create a Positive Future for the Climate, the Planet, Your Organization and Your Life*, Earthscan Publications, 2008

- Tang K. and Yeoh R., *Cut Carbon, Grow Profits - Business Strategies for Managing Climate Change and Sustainability*, Middlesex University Press, London, 2007

- Pearce D., Barbier E. and Markandya, A., *Sustainable Development: Economics and Environment in the Third World*, Earthscan Publications, London, 1990

- Steffen, A., *Worldchanging: A User's Guide for the 21st Century*, Harry N. Abrams Inc., New York, 2008

Theoretical Concepts

'Sustainable development' and 'sustainability' have become increasingly common terms widely used by corporations, pressure groups, policy makers and governments. These two buzzwords are the bottom line in business ethics, but have many definitions.

Sustainable Development – A Definition

The terms 'sustainable development' and 'sustainability' were popularised in 1987 by the World Commission on Environment and Development. According to the Brundtland Report, sustainable development meets the needs of the present without compromising the ability of future generations to meet their own needs. Sustainable development involves devising a social and economic system, which ensures that these goals are sustained, i.e. that real incomes rise, that educational standards increase, that the health of the nation improves, and that the general quality of life is advanced.[3]

The author of this Handbook identifies the potential for contradiction in this definition. According to this definition, if we look to technological and economic development in China and India, we will certainly detect a dramatic improvement although the approaches taken towards sustainable development are still in question for both. The United States of America is the leading superpower, yet is responsible for the highest per capita pollution, whose consequences are felt predominantly outside its borders.

In another definition by Pearce, sustainable development is where the costs of development are not transferred to future generations, or where they are, an attempt is made to compensate for such costs (Pearce, Barbier and Markandya, 1990).

According to the author of this handbook, sustainable development is a global strategy focused on long-term profit for all stakeholders in society, achievable by prioritising a balance between economic growth, social development and respect for nature. These are the primary objectives we have to prioritise and practice in order to either become a good corporate citizen, a good government, or a good global citizen. Leaders and policy makers should remember that sustainable development is not just a holistic approach or corporate mission; it is the only global strategy for societies to survive and succeed in the 21st century.

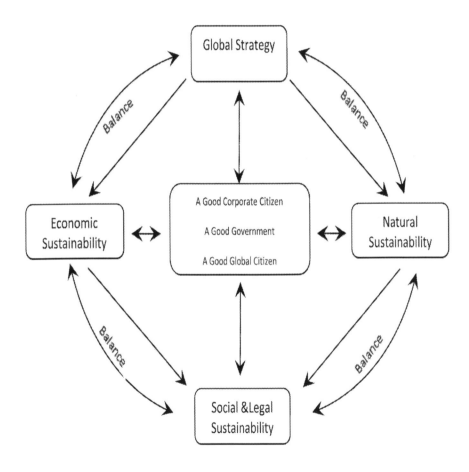

Figure 1: Global Sustainability Framework

Sustainability – A Definition

The verb 'to sustain' means to hold up; to bear; to support; to provide for or to keep going (Chambers Concise Dictionary, 2008). But it is imperative to note that sustainability does not simply involve the meaning of the root word 'sustain'. In fact, sustainability is related to the quality of lifestyle in society, where sound development of economic, social and environmental systems provide a healthy, fruitful and dignified life for all community residents, while also assuring it for future generations.

The United States Environment Protection Agency recognises the many definitions of the term 'sustainability'. Underlying these are three constant principles, 1) Balancing a Growing Economy, 2) Environmental Protection, 3) Social Responsibility. Thus in order to achieve sustainability, it is vital to implement a process of sustainable development.

Background Analysis

Vladimir Ivanovich Vernadsky was one of the pioneers of environmental science and his work remains influential today. Born in 1863 St Petersburg, Vernadsky proposed that living organisms play as important role in shaping the Earth as do physical forces, which would later inform hypotheses supporting the idea of the planet as a single living organism, such as the Gaia principle proposed by James Lovelock. In *The Biosphere*,[4] published in 1926, Vernadsky pioneered new approaches to sustainable development that emphasised the essential equilibrium that needed to be reached between human development and environmental protection.

The concept of sustainable social and economic development is now firmly on the political agenda of most developed nations, though there remains a question mark as to its effective application and practice. The role of corporations in this process emerged in the United States of America in the 1950's, a natural setting given its heavily corporate-focused social model. It was here that the importance of corporate social responsibility (CSR) and the development of its conceptual framework evolved.[5] As corporate influence has increased worldwide, this framework offers one of the most effective and relevant approaches to achieving sustainable development today.

Carroll and Buchholz[6] offer a definition of CSR as one that "encompasses the economic, legal, ethical and philanthropic expectations placed on organizations by society at a given point in time." They shaped these four interrelated aspects within a pyramid and state that true social responsibility requires the meeting of these four levels successively.

Markets work best when they are sensitive to changes in the marketplace. For business this means responding to the regulations of the marketplace and to consumer demand – whether with regard to pricing, quality, presentation or the process of manufacture. In an increasingly branded marketplace, where for businesses in this market sector image is of foremost concern, products are evaluated on a range of factors that place them in a 'setting'.

Advertisements for lifestyle brands portray an image that places the product in a particular environment that clouds out the rest of the world and entices the consumer to be a part of a particular scene. Under such a marketing strategy, which is a compact willingly entered into by corporation and consumer alike, the corporation has an undertaking, one could almost say a responsibility and duty, to ensure that the product is not demeaned by contamination with an outer world. While on the one hand this implies a certain level of secrecy surrounding the means of production, it also results in the need to maintain advertised values in the production process.

This obligation is not limited only to lifestyle brands. Many products sell themselves on virtues of honesty, protectiveness, wholesomeness, comprehensiveness, supportiveness and shared values. Such an image would be damaged by revelations about the manufacturing process that suggested the contrary.

Corporations regularly present to the consumer and their employees a manifesto of their shared beliefs, their social perspective. It seeks to present the corporation as a social unit, a living organism within a network of other organisms, usually in line with ecological thinking. Such a template presents challenges for a corporation to make the adjustments necessary to respond to the nature of the contemporary marketplace, but it also presents opportunities on a far wider scale. The business that responds best to these conditions is best able to receive its accompanying benefits.

Corporate Social Responsibility

The business model is the pre-eminent model through which most goods and services are distributed. This extends from consumer goods and financial services to the market for carbon emissions trading – a business-led solution to a global environmental problem. Similarly, there is an on-going re-prioritisation from giving aid to supporting trade in the developing world.

Corporate social responsibility theories identify the importance of the business and social environment in doing business. Institutions, infrastructure, regulation, accountability, policing, education and transparency are all vital components. It is these factors that often help to regulate the behaviour of a corporation as much as the individuals within it.

Nevertheless there will always be individuals and corporations that take a lead to set their own standards and raise those of others, such as Cadbury's and Rowntree's in the United Kingdom in the 19th century before concepts of CSR had been developed. Based upon conviction and values, corporations such as these highlight the message that extra costs entailed by CSR come with extra benefits. These may accrue in the form of a healthier and more efficient workforce, or a higher public profile and improved image in the marketplace. This is as true today as in previous decades, in spite of the growing distances placed between production and consumption, between employee and consumer.

In an age of increased public scepticism of public institutions, corporations are in a position to establish trust with society based upon the exercise of shared values. This trust is hard won and easily lost, but comes highly rewarded.

But it must be emphasised for all stakeholders, that addressing corporate social responsibility is a compact between the private and public sectors. The case of greenhouse gas emitting chlorofluorocarbons (CFCs) is worth keeping in mind. Following the discovery of the high level and persistence of CFCs in the atmosphere by James Lovelock in the early 1970's, and growing scientific evidence over the following decade of the alarming effect on the stratospheric ozone layer, a co-ordinated global approach was taken to remedy the situation. In 1987 the Montreal Protocol on Substances that Deplete the Ozone Layer called for the use of CFCs to be phased out in developed countries by 1996 and in developing countries (supported by financial assistance) by 2010. Alongside further initiatives, by 2003 the use of CFCs was reduced by 99% in the developed world and by 50% in the developing world.[7] At the same time, many corporations responded to consumer concern by voluntarily removing CFCs prior to legislated dates, strengthening a bond between corporation and consumer. The business world has also responded by developing alternatives to CFCs for use in a wide range of consumer products and scientific applications. A combination of united and coherent global regulation alongside a responsive marketplace has resulted in a highly efficient and effective response to an issue of major significance for the environment, human health and the global economy.

Acting ethically and adopting a social responsibility method inside and outside the organisation shows the divergences between management and stakeholders, though ethics is always a question mark. It is also a hot discussion issue, do business ethically or do business for business.

It is important to clarify the concept of business ethics. The term ethics originates from the Greek word 'ethikos', meaning 'character' and can be translated as 'custom', referring to the customary way humans should behave in society. Ethics is a branch of philosophy to do with morality which explores actions and consequences, motives, moral decision-making and human nature. Ethics are a relative and fluid measurement, reflecting changes in the background landscape and human culture. While certain ethical principles remain constant, such as honesty and integrity of action, factors affecting ethical judgements include levels of disposable wealth, resource availability, fashions, improved communications, availability of information and scientific discoveries.

As human populations have rapidly increased, and their output per capita has risen also, the cumulative effect of human activity has so greatly increased pressures on the environment that public awareness realises the ethical discipline required of each individual and business is much higher than would have been required given a smaller population. This argument acknowledges that greater environmental and resource pressures force individuals and businesses – without any lowering of ethical behaviour - into decisions which they would not make if such pressures did not exist.

A second explanation is that as society develops improved communications systems, a better understanding of processes, and increased transparency of business activities, it becomes cognisant of practices and its consequences of which it was previously unaware. As a result society becomes more enquiring and sceptical, and seeks to impose higher standards on businesses and other participants in the economic system.

A third factor recognises that as society becomes wealthier, and as the merits and progress of civilisation becomes a major dialogue and preoccupation within society, there is a growing expectation that actions should match these words: that civilisation should become more civilised in its relations. As a consequence the social urge for constant improvement – for instance in GDP growth, in alleviation of poverty, in better provision of services – is also seen in the desire for better standards in business and its social responsibility.

First Earth Day, 1970

Business ethics emerged as a major subject of study during the 1970s as corporate issues of advertising, product safety, environmental externalities and corruption became entrenched sources of concern for society's stakeholders. In recent time, an increasingly competitive environment affects companies in which hostility and unethical behaviour has enforced in order to obtain the organisational goals. Businesses around the world enforce diverse techniques to increase profit while ignoring basic moral principles as human rights, child labour, environmental pollution and more.

Finally, twenty million people had attended the first Earth Day on 22 April 1970 at parks, educational campuses and religious buildings across the United States.[8] Conceived by U.S. Senator Gaylord Nelson to bring together widespread support from across social divides, the weight of numbers served to highlight the deep groundswell of public support for future environmental legislation and research. And of course we have seen the positive impact of this demonstration on the Stockholm Conference in 1972.

The Stockholm Conference, 1972

The United Nations Conference on the Human Environment, held at Stockholm in 1972, was the first major international conference to meet to discuss global and environmental issues. Discussions paved the way for a declaration of principles and obligations, as well as the establishment of the United Nations Environment Programme. There were 200 specific recommendations tackling issues such as threats to biodiversity and toxic waste, and while negotiations were complex, the final agreements achieved almost all of the targets it had sought to address. Ultimately, the conference set in motion the principle and pattern of international co-operation in regulation and action on environmental degradation that exists to this day.

IUCN Conference on Conservation and Development, 1986

The International Union for Conservation of Nature (IUCN) put forward its definition of sustainable development in its 1986 Conference on

Conservation and Development in Ottawa, Canada. It revolved around five goals:

- Integration of conservation and development

- Meeting basic human needs

- The achievement of equity and social justice

- The promotion of social self-determination and cultural diversity

- The maintenance of ecological integrity

Together with the Brundtland Report which is discussed below, it has focused perspectives and policymaking along these lines ever since.

The Brundtland Commission, 1987

Formally known as the World Commission on Environment and Development, the Commission was convened in 1983 by the United Nations to establish long-term strategies and international co-operation for tackling environmental and developmental concerns.

The Brundtland Report, *Our Common Future*, was published in 1987. It sought to address the needs of sustainable development and the ways in which it could be achieved. It stressed,

> Sustainable development is development that meets the needs of the present without compromising the ability of future generations to meet their own needs. It contains within it two key concepts:
>
> - the concept of 'needs', in particular the essential needs of the world's poor, to which overriding priority should be given;
>
> - and the idea of limitations imposed by the state of technology and social organization on the environment's ability to meet present and future needs.[9]

The way to achieve it was for a new compact of co-operation by all stakeholders: governments, businesses, citizens, public institutions and civil society. This conclusion has influenced mainstream thinking, including ideas of business ethics and corporate social responsibility.

The Rio Earth Summit, 1992

Marking the twentieth anniversary of the Stockholm Conference, the United Nations Rio de Janeiro Earth Summit brought together delegates from 172 governments with the aim of developing a global approach with man and nature in symbiosis. The major agreements reached during the conference were:

- The Rio Declaration on Environment and Development [see Appendix I]

- The Convention on Biological Diversity [see Appendix II]

- The Framework Convention on Climate Change (the forerunner of the Kyoto Protocol)

- The Statement of Principles for Forest Management [see Appendix III]

- Agenda 21 – a blueprint for action for the 21st century, whose full implementation was affirmed at the Johannesburg Summit in 2002

The Johannesburg World Summit, 2002

The World Summit on Sustainable Development, held in Johannesburg in 2002, sought to lay out firm targets and strategies to back up previous declarations such as Agenda 21, bringing together tens of thousands of participants from government, business and civil society. The table below shows the key issues and elements of Agenda 21.

Elements	Issues
Social and economic dimensions to development	Poverty, Production and Consumption, Health, Human Settlement, Integrated Decision-Making

Conservation and management of natural resources	Atmosphere, Oceans and Seas, Land, Forests, Mountains, Biological Diversity, Ecosystems, Biotechnology, Freshwater Resources, Toxic Chemicals, Hazardous Radioactive and Solid Wastes
Strengthening role of major groups	Youth, Women, Indigenous Peoples, Non-Government Organisations, Local Authorities, Trade Unions, Business, Scientific and Technical Communities, Farmers
Means of implementation	Finance, Technology Transfer, Information, Public Awareness, Capacity Building, Education, Legal Instruments, Institutional Frameworks

Figure 2: Agenda 21: Elements and Issues

In May 2002, the UN Secretary General Kofi Annan introduced the framework papers for the summit, stating the intention to meet the challenges of achieving the Millennium Development Goals and caring for the planet.

> The Johannesburg Summit aims to find practical ways for humanity to respond to both these challenges – to better the lives of all human beings, while protecting the environment. The Summit also aims to move from commitments – of which we have had plenty, 30 years ago and 10 years ago - to action. I see five specific areas where concrete results are both essential and achievable.[10]

Secretary General Annan affirmed the priority of five key areas, presented in the acronym WEHAB:

• <u>Water</u> – Provide access for the more than one billion people without clean drinking water and two billion people without proper sanitation.

- <u>Energy</u> – Provide access for the more than two billion people without modern energy services; promote renewable energy; reduce over-consumption; and ratify the Kyoto Protocol to address climate change.

- <u>Health</u> – Address the effects of toxic and hazardous materials; reduce air pollution (which kills three million people each year), and lower the incidence of diseases related to water pollution and poor sanitation.

- <u>Agricultural productivity</u> – Work to reverse land degradation, which affects about two-thirds of the world's agricultural lands.

- <u>Biodiversity and ecosystem management</u> – Reverse the processes that have destroyed about half of the world's tropical rainforests and mangroves, and are threatening 70% of the world's coral reefs and decimating the world's fisheries.[11]

The Kyoto Protocol, 1997-2005

Building on the aspirations of the United Nations Framework Convention on Climate Change in reducing greenhouse gas emissions as a major source of climate change, the Kyoto Protocol laid down legally binding targets for 37 industrialised countries and the European Union. Adopted in Kyoto, Japan on 11 December 1997, the rules for implementation were established in Marrakech in 2001 and came into force on 16 February 2005.

The impetus for the Protocol was the increasing recognition of global warming as a real trend both now and in the future. The fear of rapidly increasing temperatures is that animal and plant species will be unable to adapt to changes in the short space of time and will lead to major extinction events. Another fear is that major environmental changes will result and will in turn lead to further environmental and human consequences:

- melting polar ice caps, which will further result in rising sea levels that will flood coastal regions in countries such as Bangladesh and low-lying island groups such as the Maldives

- the expansion of deserts that will encroach upon neighbouring settlements, reducing land fertility, raising land use pressures and increasing the threat of sand storms

- changes in local weather patterns such as El Nino, leading to disruptions in ecosystems around the world in a domino affect, leading to events such as the bleaching of coral reefs in the Maldives

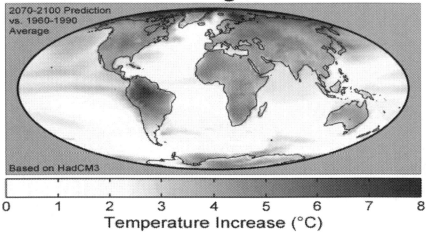

Figure 3: Global Warming Predictions, 2070-2100
Source: Robert A. Rohde, created for Global Warming Art, http://
en.wikipedia.org/wiki/File:Global_Warming_Predictions_Map.jpg

The graph above illustrates how the predicted rise in temperatures from the period 1960-90 to the period 2070-2100 will not be uniformly spread across the globe but vary from region to region, reflecting the different effects of environmental changes on local ecosystems. Nevertheless this does not imply that the consequences arising from rising temperatures will be limited to those regions experiencing the greatest increases. Regions that are predicted to experience the largest rises in temperature – the Arctic and the Amazon basin – are key regions for the stability of the global climate. The melting of the polar ice caps will flood coastal regions across the globe, while the Amazon rainforest, which is home to a large proportion of the planet's biodiversity, is also an important zone for carbon capture. Oceans, which in general are predicted to experience the smallest rises in temperatures, are acutely sensitive to these changes. Minor adjustments in temperature are enough to disrupt ocean currents that rely on temperature disparities, such as the Atlantic trade currents and the Gulf Stream, and are essential to the movements of so much life in the oceans.

In line with the Framework Convention, the Protocol accepted that the rise in human-induced greenhouse gas emissions has been responsible for the bulk of the increase in mean global temperatures over the last 50 years, that the responsibility for this lies in the hands of industrialised nations, and furthermore that these countries must take the initiative to correct the problem.

The Protocol established target reductions of on average 5% of the level of greenhouse gas emissions of countries in 1990, to be met during the five-year period from 2008 to 2012, and to be achieved primarily through national initiatives, allied with flexible additional mechanisms including a carbon market for emissions trading.

While the overall targets will, in all likelihood, be met, the impact of the Protocol is debated. The United States, the major source of emissions, failed to ratify the treaty, and Australia has failed to implement it. The reductions are not substantial and the choice of 1990 as the base year, which was a naturally high point of emissions for several countries, has added to this impression.

Moreover, the Protocol is going to end in 2012, and with unresolved disagreements, there is no clear direction for the way ahead.

Population Growth – the Raging Monster

The key reason for a lack of sustainability is the great strain placed on the planet's resources as a result of population growth. The consequences of this on food production, raw material use, high population densities, combined with a modern lifestyle that produces unrestricted non-biodegradable waste products, is clear to see, whether in landslides afflicting shanty towns or in soil degradation. With the consequence that higher birth rates eventually lead to an aging society that will place an even higher premium on birth rates, it is extraordinary that this subject has only ever been tackled seriously by the government of the People's Republic of China, with its one-child policy introduced in 1978.

The population of the world doubled from 3.2 billion in 1962 to 6.4 billion in 2005 and is forecast to grow to 9.2 billion by 2050.

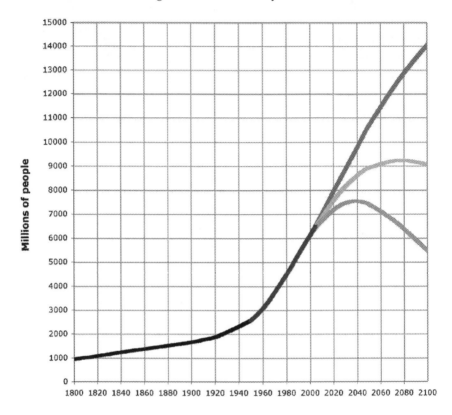

Figure 4: World Population from 1800 to 2100
[12], based on UN 2004 projections[13] (red, orange, green) and US Census Bureau historical estimates[14] (black) Source: Loren Cobb, http:// commons.wikimedia.org/wiki/File:World-Population-1800-2100.png

South Asia is one of the most populous regions in the world, and no sustainable development strategy in the region can responsibly avoid addressing this subject. According to the Department of Social and Economic Affairs of the United Nations Secretariat,[15] most countries in South Asia witnessed population growth rates of between 2-3% per annum during the second half of the 20th century, peaking in the early 1970's. Since this time rates have been steadily declining so that by the new millennium, most countries were experiencing growth rates well below 2%. Sri Lanka stands out for its long term past and projected trend of having the lowest growth rates in the region, currently 0.88% for 2005-2010, while Pakistan (2.16% for

2005-2010) and Nepal (1.85% for 2005-2010) experiencing the highest predicted rates for the coming decades.

All countries in South Asia are expected to experience declining growth rates in the coming years, on the basis of a medium variant identified by the United Nations. Actual population numbers will continue to grow overall and falling percentage increases will be of larger base numbers as a whole. In this chart, only Sri Lanka is predicted to experience population decline by the end of the period.

Managing population demographics can present an acute quandary for political leaders and policy makers. While a high population growth rate can result in a plentiful, youthful workforce, it can present difficulties for maintaining social order given insufficient employment opportunities, and it raises the spectre of a large rise in the numbers of elderly citizens in subsequent decades. A low growth rate or declining rate, on the other hand, as experienced by Japan and Russia today, presents real difficulties for sustaining an already ageing population.

In his book *The Diversity of Life*, the Pulitzer Prize-winning biologist and theorist E.O. Wilson wrote,

> The raging monster upon the land is population growth. In its presence, sustainability is but a fragile theoretical construct. To say, as many do, that the difficulties of nations are not due to people but to poor ideology or land-use management is sophistic.

> If Bangladesh had 10 million inhabitants instead of 115 million, its impoverished people could live on prosperous farms away from the dangerous floodplains midst a natural and stable upland environment. It is also sophistic to point to the Netherlands and Japan, as many commentators incredibly still do, as models of densely populated but prosperous societies. Both are highly specialized industrial nations dependent upon massive imports of natural resources from the rest of the world.

> If all nations held the same number of people per square kilometre, they would converge in quality of life to Bangladesh rather than to the Netherlands and Japan, and

their irreplaceable natural resources would soon join the Seven Wonders of the World as scattered vestiges of an ancient history.[16]

To address issues of sustainability with diligence and urgency requires tackling a many-headed hydra. It requires flexibility, bringing together many stakeholders to contribute their knowledge as well as their enterprise. It requires a fully modern approach that mirrors the modern flexible, decentralised corporate structure that encourages independent thinking, responsibility and creativity.

As the famous physicist and Nobel laureate Albert Einstein said, "The problems in the world today are so enormous they cannot be solved with the level of thinking that created them."

Energy Use – A Finite Resource

Demand and supply of oil, gas, coal, uranium, underground water and rare earth materials are forecasted to peak in coming years as reserves are depleted. At the same time the threat of climate change is putting pressure on the energy sector to move away from carbon to nuclear, solar and other environmentally friendly energy sources. Oil currently accounts for between 34% and 37% of the world's primary energy, with components of crude oil feeding the chemicals, plastics and fertiliser industries. [see Appendix IV – Oil in Numbers]

National and international efforts have been focused on the unsustainable, health damaging and environmentally deleterious production, supply and use of energy; and many lessons have been learned. Some of these efforts include the introduction of liquid petroleum gas. It offers a better way to reduce pressure on wood stocks, human work and smoke-related ills, although it does not eliminate long-term sustainability problems. The present high dependency on oil, gas and coal, which are non-renewable and sustainable, requires new wide-ranging strategies to curb their use and our oil dependency.

The Intergovernmental Panel on Climate Change warns that failure to act to reduce greenhouse gas emissions now will lead to costly risks for society, the economy and the Earth. These risks include shortages of water and extensive drought, more extreme weather events, lower yields from agriculture in already vulnerable areas, the loss of many animal and plant species, and increases in diseases.

Poorer countries are more vulnerable to the effects of climate change and are likely to suffer disproportionately, although no single country can avoid its effects. In the summer of 2007, a report by the OEDC revealed that the coverage of the Arctic Sea ice reached a new record low, opening up the Northwest Passage for the first time. It also highlighted the catastrophes of 2006, when North America and Europe suffered more droughts, heat waves and forest fires. Parts of Australia are suffering their sixth year of drought, while the European Alps suffered from record low snowfall in the prime holiday week last Christmas, with a resulting impact on local economies.[17]

The Poverty Challenge

At least 1.6 billion people still do not have access to electricity for lighting, refrigeration, mechanical power, telecommunications and other beneficial uses, though more than 1 billion people gained access to electricity during the past 25 years. Four out of five people without access to electricity live in rural areas of the developing world in South Asia and Sub-Saharan Africa. In Sub-Saharan Africa only 8% of the rural population has access to electricity, compared with 51% of the urban population. The same pattern exists in South Asia, where only 30% of the rural population has access compared with 68% of the urban population. Nearly 1.5 billion people will still lack access to electricity by 2030 if we do not make positive changes to policy and investment in energy infrastructure. In this case a major expansion of electricity supply is needed in both the urban and rural areas of these regions.[18]

The need to address sustainable development – in other words to ensure a good quality of life for all without destroying the environment or putting future generations at risk – cannot come at the expense of satisfying the basic needs of the world's poorest people. Sustainable development requires that both are achieved simultaneously and recognizes that the ends cannot be separated from the means.

A South Asian Response to Sustainable Development

Stakeholders such as academic groups in South Asia have undertaken extensive research on these issues. These include, most notably, Bangladeshi-born Nobel laureate Professor Muhammad Yunus with his contribution to microcredit and microfinance, and the Indian economist and Nobel laureate Amartya Sen, with his research into an alternative approach to human development and poverty issues. However, microfinance is not a sole solution of poverty alleviation but it can be considered one of the most effective parts of the toolbox. In fact the success depends on the ethical management style and understanding of sustainable development. The author has explained these issues in another conference paper 'Impact of Microfinance Operations on the Livelihood of the Clients: A Review of the Existing Literature'.

In India, The Energy and Resources Institute and Centre for Environmental Education have been working on sustainability issues since long before the 1992 Rio Summit, highlighting the commitment of these countries to addressing sustainability in the development of their countries. Regional co-operation is supported by initiatives including the Asian Development Bank established in 1966, and the South Asian Association for Regional Cooperation's (SAARC) Coastal Zone Management Centre, inaugurated in 2005.

On the other hand, politicians, lawyers, company directors, media gurus, actors and actresses often enjoy more importance than academics in South Asia. Consequently, well-informed academics are too often hindered in influencing policy with regard to sustainable development in any significant way. Their role remains limited to paperwork, as the political and money-focused corporate leaders have more influence on policy establishment and activation.

For much of their independent histories, the government-regulated economies of South Asia have inculcated an attitude of indifference by large and small companies towards sustainability issues. In most cases, environmental and social issues have featured low on the agenda.

Local Government Response to Sustainable Development

In the Local Government Declaration at the 2002 Johannesburg World Summit on Sustainable Development - where leaders and representatives of city and local governments across the world, supported by international and national associations agreed the importance of local government in the implementation of sustainable development - it was clearly reiterated that,

We live in an increasingly interconnected, interdependent world. The local and the global are intertwined. Local government cannot afford to be insular and inward-looking. Fighting poverty, exclusion and environmental decay is a moral issue, but also one of self-interest. Ten years after Rio, it is time for action by all spheres of government, all partners. And local action, undertaken in solidarity, can move the world.[19]

Ultimately it requires a sizeable proportion of political leaders and policy makers to grasp this model and contribute towards its realisation under the umbrella of a regional concept of sustainability. Political instability, corruption and poor law and order enforcement are key problems for the governments of most of South Asian countries. On top of these, climate change related issues such as floods, droughts, cyclones, and other extreme weather-related events are also ongoing issues. Hence, strategic co-ordination of disaster risk-management and the effects of climate-change should be at the top of their agenda. Local political representatives too often respond to issues by saying, "All depends on God. God has created us and he will manage it." In fact, by saying this they seek to avoid their responsibilities to citizens and to the wider society.

Corporations and local business people too often use their influence on government to ensure they do not focus too much on environmental and CSR issues, in order to minimise their own costs. Ship breaking is a major business supplying scrap metal in Bangladesh, India and Pakistan, yet which is banned in 190 countries. Critics say its workers face death or poisoning from toxins. Yet key stakeholders in this business ignore concerns, stating it creates job opportunities and supports recycling in the metal industry

However, some South Asian countries have recently taken strong initiatives to limit the damages caused by natural disaster. Several countries have begun to develop national-level disaster management legislation and to institutionalise national disaster management frameworks that engage district and state-level authorities in action planning to improve their resilience to natural disasters, as indicate below.

India: India has improved its ability to manage disaster. The National Disaster Management Framework (August 2004) sets out policy parameters and provides guidelines on institutional mechanisms; disaster prevention strategies; early warning systems; disaster mitigation, preparedness and response; and human resource development.

Bangladesh: Bangladesh is trying hard to improve its ability to manage disaster risks, in particular floods and cyclones, since the cyclone of 1991 that claimed nearly 140,000 lives. This has been the result of a gradual shift from a response-based approach to one that incorporates elements of greater emergency preparedness and risk mitigation. However, the Government of Bangladesh is still struggling with the long term strategy in order to handle the annual flood and its affect.

Pakistan: Because of the political instability, Pakistan is unable to implement a sustainable strategy in this particular area. However, A National Disaster Risk Management Framework, operational since March 2007, serves as a vision and provides guidelines to co-ordinate responses across sectors and stakeholders.

Sri Lanka: In July 2005, the Government of Sri Lanka introduced the Disaster Management Act No.13 in which provides the legal basis for instituting a disaster risk management system in the country. In December 2005 a separate Ministry for Disaster Management was established in order to implementation of the National Disaster Management Plan and the National Emergency Operation Plan.

Figure 5: Disaster Management Initiatives – India, Bangladesh, Pakistan & Sri Lanka

Indicators

The Environment Sustainability Index (ESI) gives a clear illustration of the capability of South Asian countries to safeguard the environment in the near future. The Environmental Sustainability Index is a survey that employs a wide range of indicators to assess the ability of each country to safeguard the environment over coming decades. Out of 146 countries surveyed in the Environmental Sustainability Index of 2005,[20] South Asian countries received the following rankings:

Country	ESI Score	ESI Rank
Afghanistan*	-	-
Bangladesh	44.1	114
Bhutan	53.5	43
India	45.2	101
Maldives*	-	-
Nepal	47.7	85
Pakistan	39.9	131
Sri Lanka	48.5	79

* not included in the study

Figure 6: Environmental Sustainability Index, 2005

In the 2010 Environmental Performance Index (EPI) report,[21] which aims to set out how each country is faring against the particular environmental issues that are confronting them, South Asian countries received the following rankings out of the 163 nations surveyed:

Country	EPI Score	EPI Rank
Afghanistan*	-	-
Bangladesh	44.0	139
Bhutan	68.0	40
India	48.3	123
Maldives	65.9	48
Nepal	68.2	38
Pakistan	48.0	125
Sri Lanka	63.7	58

* not included in the study

Figure 7: Environmental Performance Index, 2010

Microscopic View of Sustainable Development in Some Parts of South Asia

Population growth and poverty alleviation are two of the main priorities in most countries in South Asia. Large population growth has a direct impact on resource use and nutritional and health issues, which create pressures on natural ecosystems and natural resources. The table below shows the population, density and GDP per capita of countries in South Asia.

Country	Area (km2)	Population (2009)	Density (/km2)	Nominal GDP (2009)	GDP per capita (2009)
Afghanistan	647,500	33,609,937	52	$14,044 million	$486
Bangladesh	147,570	162,221,000	1,099	$94,507 million	$551
Bhutan	38,394	697,000	18	$1,269 million	$1,832
India	3,287,240	1,198,003,000	365	$1,235,975 million	$1,122
Maldives	298	396,334	1,330	$1,357 million	$4,388
Nepal	147,181	29,331,000	200	$12,615 million	$427
Pakistan	803,940	180,808,000	225	$166,515 million	$981
Sri Lanka	65,610	20,238,000	309	$41,323 million	$2,068

Figure 8: South Asian Regional Data
Source: http://en.wikipedia.org/wiki/South_Asia

There are different definitions as to which countries comprise the region of South Asia. According to The World Bank, South Asia is defined as including India, Pakistan, Bangladesh, Sri Lanka, the Maldives, Nepal, Bhutan and Afghanistan. Other definitions sometimes include Iran, Burma or the British Indian Ocean Territory.

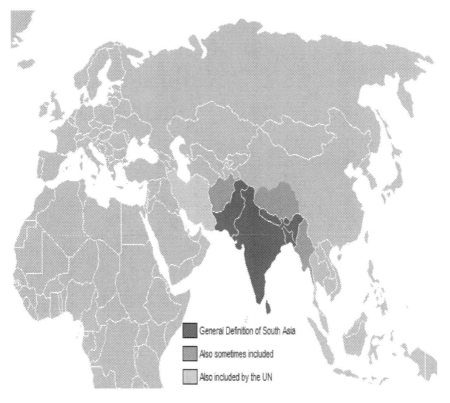

Figure 9: Map of South Asia Featuring Extended Definitions
Source: http://en.wikipedia.org/wiki/File:South_Asia_(ed)update.PNG

Most of the poor in South Asia live in rural areas and many depend on agriculture for their livelihood, which is susceptible to variations in weather patterns and changes in other environmental processes, such as irrigation systems. During a visit to Patbaria, a village in Bangladesh situated on the banks of the river Padma, in January 2010, the author questioned a number of farmers on their lifestyles, livelihoods and economic situation. They answered, "Our present and future depends on nature." This simple answer raises the question, 'Which are the influential groups affecting nature's processes?' Most villagers' incomes, lifestyles and spending power fluctuate from one season to another, with other sources of uncertainty resulting from the spread of various types of diseases, political unrest and natural disaster.

Most parts of the South Asia used to experience six seasons a year. The author has interviewed a number of students and citizens from Bangladesh, India, Pakistan and Sri Lanka regarding their recent experiences of six seasons (see figure 10). Most answered that changes of six seasons are now childhood memories, that they rarely feel it anymore. They now perceive there to be four seasons (summer, the rainy period, winter and spring).

Season	Characteristics
Summer (March to May)	• The heat starts intensifying more rapidly • The soil turns dusty and almost white • There is lightning, thunderstorms and hail • The rivers dry out • It is the peak time for the brick industry, because of the temperature
Monsoons (June to August)	• The rains are at first a welcome relief from the baking, dusty hot season • The land turns into a brown and watery mass, ever changing in shape and texture • Fields and homes are flooded, people and animals have to move to higher ground. Many people move from the village to the town for safety, often living in slums or on the street. • During the rains, most villages are isolated, accessible only by boat • Children leap naked into ponds • The beauty of rains and water also inspire the poetry, art and songs of the people

Autumn (September to October)	• The skies are blue and a cool wind blows • Flowers bloom, the rice ripens and the harvest begins • Blue, gold and green are the colours of Autumn – blue sky, golden sun and green vegetation from emerald to jade, pea to lime, shamrock to sea-green • There is a slight chill late at night and the air is a bit humid
Late Autumn (October to November)	• The land is at its luscious best. Festivals flourish to hail the harvest, the end of the floods, the coming of the new soil and the wonder of the rivers. • Villagers dressed in bright clothes and singing for money • The flowers bloom – jasmine, water lily, rose, magnolia, hibiscus and bougainvillea • The air is no longer humid. Fresh scents replace the dry jute smell. • It marks the start of the wedding season where receptions are held under red, blue, green or white tents
Winter (November to December)	• The weather becomes more arid and less humid. Winter in South Asia is usually mild and enjoyable in comparison to winters elsewhere. • The land dries and dust forms • People wear warm clothes, though poor people suffer in the cold weather • Green and seasonal vegetables are available in everywhere
Spring (December to February)	• Flowers blooming, birds singing, nights and early mornings are chilly • The countryside hums with fairs, parades and commemorations. Arts festivals celebrate painting and handicrafts, poetry, music and drama. • It is the bearer of news for social and cultural festivals with a frantic whirl of invitations to weddings, parties and dinners

Figure 10: The Traditional Six Seasons of South Asia

The Indian Government's 10th Plan has set its sights on achieving a rate of growth of 8% in order to tackle poverty and achieve human development targets. While improvements have been made, there remain relatively unfavourable international comparisons regarding infectious diseases and gender-related issues such as mortality rates in childbirth and gender imbalances amongst students in secondary education.

In Bangladesh, in the early years of the millennium, 46.5% of people were classed as living below the poverty line, down from 70.6% in 1973-4. The government sought to halve this further by 2010, while also addressing issues of governance, growth and social development.[22]

In Bhutan, the government has set itself the goal of achieving universal primary education, compared to 67% in 1990 and 72% in 2000. At the same time it is focusing on a wide range of social and health improvements, while health care coverage exists for 90% of the population.[23]

The Human Development Index is a measure adopted by the United Nations Development Programme to assess countries relating to the economic well-being, health and education of their citizens. Of South Asian countries, Sri Lanka is ranked highest at 91 in 2010[24], with the Maldives at 117. From 2007[25] to 2010, India made progress rising to 199 from 127th place. Over the same period, Pakistan rose to t he rank of 125 from 135, and Bangladesh to 129 from 139. Nepal is placed at 138 in 2010 and Bhutan, although receiving no rating that year, was ranked at 134 in 2007.

South Asia suffers from a high sensitivity to natural disasters, caused by the natural characteristics of its ecosystems, the concentration of high-density populations, relative poverty and the presence of formidable geological formations such as the Himalayas and large river systems.

The Himalayas provide water to half the world's population. But these populations are also dependent on its glacial water melt during the dry season, which are threatened by global warming. As well as reducing the long-term availability of this annual resource, melt water flooding is increased in the short term. This presents a major challenge to agriculture in the region, which remains the most significant source of employment and income.

The localised threats to agriculture from climate change will however differ from region to region, depending on the local climate and the dependence on particular crops.

In a study undertaken by The World Bank,[26] over the period from 1990-2008, natural disasters were reported to have affected a cumulative total of almost 146 million people in Bangladesh and 885 million people in India, respectively by far the greatest tolls in terms of percentage of the population affected of all countries in the region. Another 6.3 million people in Sri Lanka, 28 million in Pakistan and 5.4 million people in Afghanistan were also affected during this time frame. Collectively, US$ 44,787,984 million worth of damage was recorded[27]

CASE STUDIES

Sustainable Development in Bangladesh

No one country is alike. While differences exist due to human developments - affecting political, military, scientific and cultural affairs and the development of supporting institutions - historical and anthropological evidence, as well as common sense, also points to the involvement of non-human factors such as fertility of the soil, climactic conditions and availability of particular livestock and crops.

If we look at the current pattern of trade in the world economy we will see each country plays a different part in supply and demand. This depends on various components such as historical and economic characteristics, technological development, geography, the creativity of the people, the availability of raw materials for particular productions and many more things besides. In the case of Bangladesh, because of a vast cheap and skilled labour force, it is a key player in the ready-made garment export industry. Nevertheless it follows a strong historical connection, with Dhaka having been at the forefront of the global muslin trade during the 17th century when under Mughal rule.

Bangladesh is one of the most densely populated countries in the world. In terms of population it is the 8th largest nation and 93rd largest by land area. The people of Bangladesh suffer from air, water and noise pollution, especially in major urban areas. Its coastal zone, ranged across one of the largest delta regions in the world, is low lying, flat and criss-crossed by hundreds of rivers and channels. Geologists and environmentalists predict that one-third of Bangladesh will be under the sea level in 50 years' time due to rising sea levels caused by climate change. Other major environmental problems facing Bangladesh include deforestation, deteriorating water quality, natural disasters, land degradation, salinity, unplanned urbanisation, and the discharge of untreated sewage and industrial wastes.

While Government policies exist to tackle some of the problems mentioned, an absence of a defining long-term strategy, as well as a need to work closely with neighbours to address issues that traverse national borders, lead to questions regarding their implementation and monitoring.[28]

The Garment Industry

At the time of independence 1971, Bangladesh's economy depended on industries such as paper, tea, jute and fisheries, which, due to political reasons, subsequently failed to develop. The figurehead of this decline was the Adamjee Jute mill, the largest of its kind in Asia, which suffered a slow decline until its eventual closure in 2002.

However, following changes in world trade, the garment industry emerged as the fastest growing industrial sector in Bangladesh, leading the economy since the 1990's. Accounting for 80% of total exports and the largest employer in the formal sector outside of agriculture, the garment industry is seen as contributing to poverty reduction and providing employment opportunities for poor and less educated people who would otherwise be engaged in less profitable activities in rural areas. At the same time it is true to say that most of the people involved in the garment trade are not aware of issues relating to environmental pollution, corporate social responsibility and ethical business practices that should be as much a part of the industry as the making of clothes.

Issues of Corporate Social Responsibility

Given lax national controls over trade, consumer and retailer demands form the key influence on the size and the location of the garment and textile industries in different parts of the world. Since the 1980's the nature of garment retailing has changed substantially in Europe, with retailers focusing ever-greater attention on market segmentation, with targeting based on age, psychology, aspiration and income groups. This development has implications for garment manufacturers.

Style, image and marketing are readily disassociated from the physical aspect of manufacturing. The former (the value added, creative aspect) remain the preserve of the wealthy nations where the product is targeted, while the latter (the cost-based, non-creative aspect) is exported for overseas production. Thus it is image and price that form the key components of the high volume garment industry.

In the manufacturing process, given the cheap cost of the raw materials involved, it is the workforce that comes to comprise the significant cost. Peter Dicken, author of *Global Shift Transforming the World Economy*, has written, "There is no doubt that labour costs are the most significant production factors in the ready made garment industry, whereas labour costs are the most geographically variable of production costs of factories."[29]

Given this cost, an untrained workforce with few employment rights, minimal corporate social responsibility, and negligible enforcement of workplace law, many workers in garment factories in Bangladesh suffer from haphazard payment of their salaries. Employees are demotivated due to the low rates of pay, long hours and unhealthy work places and practices.

During one visit to Bangladesh, the author spoke with twenty-five workers from small and large-scale garment factories. The author asked a few common questions to every one, such as 'Do you enjoy your work?' and 'Why do you work in a factory?' Twenty responded with the same answer, that they do not enjoy working in the garment industry, but have no other choice, unless they chose to pull rickshaws. Some of the women said that before working in the garment industry they worked at home as a maidservant. They favourably compared the limited freedom in this job with that of being a maidservant.

Nevertheless, in a sweatshop workers are made to labour for over seventy or eighty hours per week and are bullied by senior managers to lie about pay and conditions. In return they often earn 25 to 30 cents an hour and risk their lives in factories where the owners lock emergency exits. Staff often work overtime with irregular payment or sometimes unpaid and risk being threatened with dismissal if they refuse.[30]

In conducting research in Bangladesh, the author found facilities provided by factory owners that did not meet either national or international health and safety standards. Moreover the government has no strong or dedicated department to work actively to legislate and enforce health and safety regulations. One such example is found in the bleaching and dyeing sector, where chemical and other toxic materials are handled without proper protection or safety guidelines. Most of the time, the safe operation of machinery is learnt from previous experience or watching others at work.

If we look at some core International Labour Organization (ILO) conventions [see Appendix V], we will realise that many of them are not followed by the ready-made garment industry in Bangladesh. Only a few manufacturers try to follow a few rules in order to satisfy foreign buyers and to avoid undue pressures from civil society groups should conditions be exposed.

Environmental Issues

In developed countries there is a strong awareness of the fragility of the local environment and the need for careful use of chemicals and toxins. This is built on a general prosperity, strong civil institutions and a moderately effective enforcement procedure. This same situation cannot be said to exist in developing countries in South Asia.

The various sectors within the garment industry, including textile mills and dyeing, printing and finishing units, handle substantial quantities of chemicals, raw materials and toxic waste.[31] With the country criss-crossed by river channels, most factories are situated on their banks,[32] and instead of managing or recycling the waste, find it simpler and cheaper to discharge it into the river. The stages of textile production comprise fibre production (fibre processing and spinning); yarn preparation; fabric production; bleaching, dyeing and printing; and finishing. Each stage produces waste that requires proper management.

At present, most private and government factories have no proper waste management or recycling systems in place. Despite the implementation in February 1995 of the Environmental Protection Act (EPA), environmental issues are not prioritised by Bangladesh's manufacturers. In a joint report by the Department of Environment, the Ministry of Industry, and the Asian Development Bank on pollution in Bangladesh, the major polluting sectors identified were paper and pulp, clothing and textile, and tanneries. The clothing and textile industries were noted as bearing a considerable responsibility for water, air, soil and surface pollution.

Water Pollution

Increasing numbers of factories in the clothing and textile sectors in Bangladesh have a negative effect on the quality of its water. The pollution from this sector has reached alarming levels as, with most of the industrial units of ready-made garment sector located along riverbanks, wastage from raw materials and finished products are disposed directly into the river. These discharges comprise complex hazardous chemicals, both organic and inorganic, mixed into bodies of water usually without treatment. Just under half of industrial locations are in the North Central region, of which one third are textile and finished garment manufacturers. Half of these are located in the Dhaka district alone, the country's capital.

Air Pollution

Most factory owners in the textile and clothing sectors do not follow any systematic approach to controlling air pollution with respect to emissions from the dyeing and bleaching activities. Dust created by cotton waste pollutes air, which is often a cause of breathing disorders, asthma and heart disease.

On the other hand, unplanned brick-fields are also polluting the environment both in the cities and villages. The Government of Bangladesh has introduced the Brick Burning Act, dictating that every chimney in a brick-field must be 50 feet high and prohibiting brick burning within five kilometers of government natural reserves. Nevertheless, owners often do not adhere to these statutes, while the accompanying growth in urbanisation to house and serve the workforce compounds local pollution and results in the destruction of natural ecological systems that can filter externalities.

Soil Pollution

The rural economy comprises a major portion of the national economy, primarily involving the agriculture of crops, livestock, fisheries and forestry. Many in the rural population are actually or nominally landless, owning less than 0.05 of an acre of land, and lack adequate knowledge of issues relating to modern land and waste management, damage to ecosystem services from human constructions, efficient irrigation systems, unsustainable consumption of biomass, and fertiliser and pesticide use.

In Bangladesh, most industrialists have no specific plans for dealing with solid waste, with manufacturers often dumping waste in low hollows, open spaces or nearby village areas. While undertaking primary research, the author found that local people blame industry for dumping chemical waste, cotton, plastics and other solid materials that damage the fertility of the soil and also make the land unfit for building development. But at the same time, common people also dump their household waste in the nearby open spaces, rivers, lakes, canals or ponds.

In earlier periods, when waste was minimal, less toxic and biodegradable, such practices could be logical or harmless - even beneficial in the case of biodegradable waste. However there is now a need to explain why the continuation of such practices is no longer suitable or beneficial, requiring new practices and infrastructure that adjust to the new externalities involved in consumption. Initiatives should be implemented to address the fact that a large proportion of the population is uninterested in recycling or waste management. No proper studies or research have so far been conducted to look into solutions for this problem.

Conclusion

In view of the growing threat to the longer-term sustainability of agriculture and natural resources, there is a need to design and enforce policies and institutional frameworks for ecosystem and natural resource management and conservation. This will be crucial to sustaining high agricultural growth in a country like Bangladesh, where the economy is fragile and the population density is especially high.

Sustainable Development in India (with the co-operation of Priyanka Taunk)

The developing world is the biggest driver of population and economic growth in the world today. It is also witnessing the great social upheaval of rapid urbanisation caused by a migration of people from rural areas to metropolitan cities in the search for work. By the year 2025, about 60% of the world's population will be living in urban areas. In 2003, 38% of Asia's population (around 1.2 billion) lived in cities, but by 2020 the urban population will have reached over 2.1 billion.[33] By some estimates at least 153 cities in Asia will have populations exceeding one million inhabitants.

The increase in vehicle numbers will outstrip even the urban population growth, leading to a corresponding increase in vehicle use and transportation and pollution concerns. While industry is seen as a major factor in pollution, transportation is a significant contributor to poor air quality and climate change. According to research undertaken by The World Bank in 2004,[34] Delhi recorded the second highest levels of particulate matter, below Cairo, followed by Kolkata in 3rd place, and Kanpur and Lucknow in joint 6th place.

At present, just under a quarter of India's total land area comprises forested areas, which is second only to agriculture. Roughly 275 million of the rural poor depend on forests for their survival and livelihoods, from such products as fodder, fruits, flowers and medicinal plants, while over two-thirds of the entire rural population rely on fuel wood for their energy needs. Forests are not only a resource, but also a home to half of India's 89 million tribal population who dwell at their fringes, sustaining cultural as well as economic ties within a subtle and complex, yet mutually beneficial, relationship.[35]

Environmental Sustainability

Considering the Indian population and its rapid economic growth in recent times, the need for environmental sustainability has gained in importance as awareness has grown of the potential negative consequences environmental degradation and unsafe practices may have on future economic prosperity, as well as to living standards and the environment. There has been an increasing emphasis by individual companies and government to adopt more sustainable procedures.

India came second in the 2008 Greendex survey of sustainable consumption, which ranks the performance of individual consumers rather than governments, and is based on transportation choices, use of green products, awareness of various environmental issues, and energy use and its conservation.[36] It can be noted here that surveys conducted in such areas as the poorer districts of Mumbai highlight the extraordinary levels of recycling undertaken through necessity and for profit creation, which far outstrip even the highest levels in developed countries. Such recycling is derived from conditions in which materials are scarce and valuable, as opposed to a general situation in the developed world where such materials hold only a negligible cost, and therefore only a negligible value.

Nevertheless, large parts of the country, especially in rural areas remain unaware of the extent of this issue, of the key state of affairs regarding local pollution and bad business practice, and of the best ways to protect their local environment.

According to The Blacksmith Institute and published by Time Magazine,[37] two places in India featured in the top ten most polluted environments on Earth in 2006. The third most polluted place in the world was calculated to be Sukinda, the site for unregulated open-pit chromite mining and processing, and estimated to potentially affect 2.5 million people. Here hexavalent chromium levels in 60% of the drinking water are twice international standards, and 84.75% of deaths in the area are attributed to chromite-related diseases. At fourth on the list is the town of Vapi, which sits at the edge of a chain of industrial estates stretching for 400km and suffers from the resulting pollution fall-out. Mercury levels in the groundwater are 96 times the safety levels recommended by the World Health Organization and abnormal levels of heavy metal traces are present in the atmosphere and are filtered through the local food chain.

These are the direct outcomes of industrial practices that have not included the externalities inherent in the industrial process within their cost structure. These costs are borne, not by the profit-making private enterprise, but by local communities and ecosystems that share little in the wealth creation.

It must be stated here that it is the responsibility of not only the Indian government, but also of private companies, institutions and citizens, to take the steps required to develop plans of action to ensure the responsible and long-term stewardship of the environment - which is not only our home, but the resource upon which all economic activity is dependent.

As it is rightly said, the young generation of today are the future leaders of tomorrow and they can have a positive impact on the future by what they do today. There are many educational institutes and colleges that have begun to emphasise the importance of environmental sustainability.

One such endeavour has been suggested by my student Priyanka Taunk, whose school, the Sacred Heart Convent School in Jamshedpur, has an Environmental Club educating students on how to protect and care for the environment. Various activities and stage skits related to environment protection and reducing inefficient electrical use are some of the key characteristics of this club, providing practical measures in daily life to conserve their impact on the environment. In this way the school believes that by instilling such values in the students from the very start, and showing how they can have actual and visible results, they will have an impact on their actions for the rest of their lives.

Corporate Social Responsibility

The Asian Sustainability Rating is a benchmarking tool for environmental, social and governance performance based on corporate disclosure of risk, undertaken by Responsible Research and CSR Asia.[38] This is a useful indicator as fundamental to corporate social responsibility is the disclosure of information and the ability of all stakeholders - whether they be shareholders, governmental authorities or local populations - to place their trust in this information. Out of the ten leading Asian economies studied, India was ranked second in 2010, up from fourth place achieved in the 2009 survey.

Corporate social responsibility is the responsibility of every company towards the community, the environment, and all those affected by the production process, whether directly or indirectly. Corporations have an ever-increasing influence and effect on society, and therefore also an increasing responsibility towards it. The Indian government has realised this and has recently attempted to draw up various guidelines on corporate social responsibility, as for instance in contributing towards a sustainable environment through proscriptions against excessive water and energy use, and encouragement to reduce waste and increase recycling. Various policies have been framed to promote the adoption of cleaner production methods and the introduction of energy efficient technologies.

Today, private companies are more involved in CSR activities than government organisations and publicly owned corporations. According to a research study of three hundred companies in 2009, CSR activities had been undertaken in twenty states. Community welfare topped the charts of under twenty-six different CSR themes initiated by these companies, with environmental and public health issues ranking next in the list.

India is one of the fastest growing economies of this century and every day we see new mergers and acquisitions of national and multinational firms. It is worth pointing out that along with steady economic growth, India is also encountering issues such as population growth, corruption, poverty and illiteracy. These need to be addressed as they directly affect not only future economic capacity but also the capacity of the environment to support and provide for this economic transformation. Companies today are aware of factors that need to be given highest priority and are coming up with ways to create awareness amongst the masses and to take the initiative through their CSR strategies. Many have recently adopted their own defined approaches towards society and the environment, and here notable successes have been achieved by companies such as Tata Group, Infosys, ITC Welcome Group, Indian Oil and Bharti Enterprises.

Below are some of the corporate and government initiatives undertaken:

- The State-owned Coal India Ltd invested US$67.5 million in 2010/11 towards social and the environmental causes.

- The Tata Group has adopted the environmental procedures laid down by Global Reporting Initiative, which functions under the guidance of United Nations. Undertakings include the regular planting of trees, the maintaining of ecological sanctuaries, the implementation of more efficient water and land use procedures, and the protection of forested areas.[39]

Its commitment to the industrial city of Jamshedpur and its surrounding villages is seen in Tate Group's construction of a hospital for residents. According to the Government of India's National Urban Sanitation Policy, Jamshedpur was ranked the 7th cleanest city in the country even though it is home to the industrial activity of Tata Steel.[40]

Lakshmi Mittal, Chairman and Chief Executive of Arcelor Mittal, praised Tata's efforts in this area, writing,

> Very few people know that Jamshedpur has been selected as a UN Global Compact City, edging out the other nominee from India, Bangalore. Selected because of the quality of life, because of the conditions of sanitation and roads and welfare. If this is not a tribute to industrial India, then what is? ... My submission to those who use phrases such as 'feel-good' and 'India Shining' is first visit Jamshedpur to understand what it all means. See Tata Steel in action to know what companies can do if they wish to. And what corporate India needs to do... Corporate India can do it but most of the time is willing to shy away. For those corporate leaders who are happier winning awards and being interviewed on their choice of clothes, my advice is visit Tata Steel, spend some days at Jamshedpur and see a nation's transformation.

- The Indian government is also making efforts to ensure that various public sector companies become involved in CSR activities, declaring mandatory contributions of 2% of the net profits from the public oil companies will go to CSR activities.[41]

- The Indian conglomerate ITC Ltd, is committed to being carbon, water, and solid waste recycling positive. A recent initiative taken by this group is the 'e-choupal', which aims to help tackle the challenges of the agricultural sector in India, which is characterised by fragmentation of farms, and poor infrastructure and facilities. In recent years, this model has expanded across all the parts of India and now covers almost three million villagers.[42]

- The Times Foundation was set up by The Times Group in 2000 with a view to give something back to society under the auspices of its various corporate social responsibility and sustainable development activities. It has also conducted workshops to educate and highlight the importance of corporate social responsibility among corporations and government institutions.[43]

- Infosys, an IT solutions and software provider, has been carrying out CSR activities through its various development centres, supporting the activities of NGOs and other institutions involved in welfare and education. Its project 'Ozone' aims to spread the awareness of issues surrounding environmental protection, while at the same time seeking to improve its own energy conservation measures and its water and waste management systems.[44]

- International companies have supported these initiatives with undertakings of their own, as with the 'Road to Zero' project by Sony. The company has also established a programme called Green Management 2010 through which it will take initiatives to reduce global warming, ensure the proper usage and disposal of chemical wastes, and increasing recycling of resources. These initiatives are being rigorously undertaken and have led to a 17% reduction in emissions of CO_2 from its business sites.

Yet while considerable efforts have been made by various large firms and government institutions in India there is still much more that needs to be done, including a committed action to encourage and harness similar efforts by smaller companies.

Even though the Indian economy is currently booming and there are a high number of small and medium size businesses trading effectively, there is little awareness of CSR among them or amongst their employees. There arises a need to spread the awareness of this issue among the small firms and help them perform their responsibilities towards society and the environment.

Even in large corporations, the importance of corporate social responsibility should be made familiar to all employees, so that it becomes an integral aspect within all their activities. If the modern corporate world relies on creative thinking and the inspiration of its workforce, then it is important that corporate social responsibility is not an afterthought or a mystery in their thinking.

Sustainable Development in the Maldives (with the co-operation of Danny Winkler)

The Republic of Maldives comprises a chain of 26 coral atolls comprising some 1,190 islands in the Indian Ocean, rising no more than 2.3 metres above sea level at any point. Given its geographical isolation and the generally small size of each island, it remains relatively dislocated from world trade, with an economy based on high-end tourism and fishing.

The main factors that need to be address by any sustainable development proposal in the country are the nation's isolation, distances between atolls, increasing population densities and rising sea levels. The Maldives is at the forefront of international efforts to protect low-lying islands states, but it remains most at risk from rising sea levels, which has focused national efforts on securing alternative homelands.

The future of the Maldives is precariously balanced. Its present situation places it at the forefront of environmental and human changes over recent decades, benefiting from tourism as a paradise island location and yet at the mercy of the same forces that created them (not only from its naturally precarious location, but also from the greenhouse gas emissions from (the still heavily subsidised) air travel industry upon which its tourism relies).

Its dependence on a narrow source of income from tourism and fisheries can be a source of concern. While tourism remains a success story, the bleaching of 90% of its coral reefs in 1998 due to an El Nino event that caused sea temperatures to rise 2 degrees centigrade over a sustained period, illustrates the country's economic fragility to future environmental shocks. While the reefs slowly recovered over the following decade, in the early part of 2010 rising ocean surface temperatures registering 1 degree centigrade above the average once again killed off the majority of reefs, which are the foundation of the country's marine ecosystem.

The Tsunami in 2004 further highlighted potential dangers, although in this case, the very fact of being small islands offering little in the way of resistance to the power of the waves, enabled the tsunami to wash over the islands with relatively little damage in relation to the scale of the event.

Environmental Challenges

Putting rising sea levels to one side, the Maldives faces specific environmental challenges. A growing population has exerted obvious pressures as the country is comprised mostly of small islands that cannot support the surge in population numbers. Nowhere is this more keenly felt than in the capital island of Male, which has turned to land reclamation in order to housing its burgeoning numbers. The island today would be literally unrecognisable for citizens of a century ago. Not only would they be unable to recognise buildings and landmarks, but would struggle to identify the island at all.

Increased populations put greater stress on ecosystem resources. While not suffering extremes of poverty as in many of the world's poorest countries, access to food presents unique logistical challenges. The small land size of most islands, traditionally covered by trees, leaves little capacity for crop production. Additionally, the general poor quality of soil, which contains a high composition of sand, severely depresses agricultural yields.

A typical case study of the agricultural challenges faced by development organisations can be found in Thinadoo, a tiny island within the smallest atoll in the country, Vaavu Atoll, where the United Nations Development Programme (UNDP) launched a project to develop domestic agriculture across what is no more than a small field. Given the particularly unfavourable soil conditions, composed heavily of sand, the project ended in failure. It would be instructive to know the full extent of prior investigation by experts before selecting the components of the project, as the land, though highly unsuitable for most crops, would doubtless support certain native crops.

The absence of transparency and openness make it difficult to assess and learn from the results of past projects. A consequence of this failure and the ongoing difficulties for the dwindling population to sustain themselves does little to prevent its continuing slide into a ghost island, comprised of the elderly and very young, as those of working age seek employment elsewhere.

The local diet remains reliant on the traditional work of fishing. This industry has sought to keep pace with the global marketplace, introducing larger mechanised ships and sea farms, catering for a variety of markets, from high volume tuna to more highly prized specialities. National and international support has assisted in some of these developments.

New Practices, New Awareness

Nevertheless there has been a slow introduction of processed foods accompanied by packaging, which has caused new problems. The packaging consists of plastics, metals and glass, and along with oil resulting from ship mechanisation has led to issues of pollution and disposal. In Vaavu Atoll, which provides a typical example, garbage disposal has become a major issue, with litter either disposed on the beaches or in a dedicated dump. These dumps are typically located on beaches and as they encroach over the water line, create hazards spilling into the ocean and impeding the natural flow of currents, with subsequent implications for beach erosion. Once pristine beaches have become hazardous areas littered at every step with plastics and broken glass. The problem has been caused, not by a sudden laxity of islanders in disposing of rubbish, but by the introduction of unfamiliar and previously unknown packaging that is non-biodegradable. Traditional waste disposal in small island nations involves disposing of (typically food) remains on the beach or in the ocean. When this was biodegradable and of a minimal quantity this proved no problem. Now attitudes have to change as islanders realise that they must act in new ways to match changing consumption patterns.

Summary of Successful Development Interventions

Given the Maldives' access to marine resources it is well placed to take advantage of potentially ecologically friendly marine business. "We rely on marine resources for most of our everyday lives," said Hussain Manik, Pearl

Culture field officer, Felidhoo, "This is a good way of making sustainable use of them."[45]

To this effect the UNDP oversaw a pearl culture project in partnership with the Maldives Marine Research Centre and funded by the Japanese Human Resource Development Fund, as a forerunner to developing local expertise in growing pearl oysters. The industry is renewable and ecologically sound and offers a new revenue source for a country dependent on concentrated income streams. As the Project Officer Hussain Mohammed explained, "If the people can sell these shells to craftsmen in these islands then they can make a handsome profit. And then the souvenir shops can sell the Maldivian handicrafts that tourists really want."[46]

Projects such as these highlight the value of, and scope for, well-directed projects, often with small budgets that provide a very real benefit for people and the environment in which they live.

Other UNDP projects in Vaavu Atoll that have had similar benefits include a micro-finance Atoll Community Development Fund, providing seed finance to local inhabitants to support small enterprises, and the provision of subsidised drinking water tanks that significantly reduced water-borne diseases amongst the atoll's population.

Unintended Consequences

As will be discussed later in the chapter 'Managing Changing Ecosystems', ecological action is beset by the problem of unintended consequences resulting from insufficient knowledge of the causes and effects within ecosystems. This becomes readily apparent in the following example from Vaavu Atoll.

Its islands, as with all those in the Maldives, are constantly shifting according to the motions of the ocean currents upon sandbanks and beaches. The beaches retreat or advance, in some cases noticeably changing the shape of islands over a period of a few decades. On the Vaavu island of Felidhoo, the construction of a jetty magnified existing erosion patterns by fracturing wave flows and creating pressure points at specific landmarks, resulting in excessive localised beach erosion. This is an immediate problem for residents tend to live close to the narrow beachfronts. Given a lack of financial and material resources, and the continuing shadow of rising levels in the long-term, the solution is often to cement existing beach lines with concrete and rocks. While effective, it destroys the natural aesthetic beauty of the area.

While the severity of the erosion and its implications for people living in its midst should not be in doubt, it does raise a serious question – what should be the limits on the destruction of nature? For most areas in the world the decision is not so stark – the region may not hold such aesthetic beauty and the efforts to correct the problem may not entail such a deterioration of its attributes. But this specific situation in the Maldives magnifies the question, and it asks us to face stark choices. Will we do *anything* to preserve our way of life over the ways of the world? And is this defensible?

Managing Sustainable Development Programmes

The question that development authorities have to ask themselves is how to continue implementing successful projects without also devoting time and money to projects that are unsuitable to local needs and unimplementable given local conditions. For every successful project in Vaavu Atoll (developing pearl culture, introducing safe drinking water, revamping the electricity network on the capital island of Felidhoo, introducing a community development fund) there are also failed projects (an unfeasible local recycling scheme in a country without recycling capacity, a failed agricultural project in Thinadoo, construction of jetties and sea defences with unintended consequences) all of which could have been prevented with better co-ordination between locals and experts.

It surely cannot be acceptable that donor countries' funds, and the efforts and resources of the recipient nation, are devoted to projects that are wasteful and disruptive to the local economy and environment. It is a perennial problem, whose answer can be found partly in better knowledge, communication and systems, but also in the involvement of individuals who refuse to accept mediocre results and who seek to implement projects on a perceptive and imaginative level.

For the success of all projects, be they developmental, ecological or entrepreneurial, depend on the individual as well as the setting. It is why the choice of individual is imperative, as is the involvement of stakeholders to provide the counterbalance to the efforts and decisions of the organising authorities.

The example of one of the author's friend (Danny Winkler), who worked on United Nations projects in Vaavu Atoll, is illustrative of this choice. Enrolled originally to work on a Beach Erosion project and Garbage Disposal project, the original proposals were found to be unimplementable and without bearing to the conditions on the ground. While surveying the atoll and drawing up new proposals for both, he worked independently on projects that included proposals to redevelop the electricity grid of Felidhoo, to create a mobile library for the atoll's schools, to secure more staff and facilities for the atoll's health centre, and to draw up repayment systems for a new Community Development Fund.

For all efforts to promote systems, they are only as good as the individuals who staff them. Sustainable development approaches must seek to withdraw from the bureaucratic model based on hierarchies and become more flexible in their approach, in a manner reflecting modern creative business models. Our justification is that solutions must be creative; they must be ingenious. Why attempt to prevent beach erosion with concrete when you could do the job with tree planting, which also comes with additional benefits?

The reader is again referred to the quote of Albert Einstein, because it is worth repeating, and worth acting upon, "The problems in the world today are so enormous they cannot be solved with the level of thinking that created them." Einstein is not suggesting alternative thinking, but an alternative *level* of thinking. The world has continued, in general, to ignore these words, and it has, in general, continued to act in the same way and suffer the same problems. South Asia is at the forefront on an emerging new world. It is for South Asia to adopt a new mantle, to be brave and ambitious, and to welcome a new *level* of thinking and a global strategy.

Sustainable Development in Pakistan

The United Nations's Human Development Report[47] places Pakistan 101st in the Human Poverty Index, with 60.3% of the country's population below the poverty line. Of those in poverty, some 80% are from rural areas with an average annual income of the equivalent of US$400.[48]

Despite recent political instability, there has been economic development in the past decade. Yet this has been accompanied by increasing inequality, particularly in rural regions, which continue to suffer from a lack of resources in education and health sectors, and in basic infrastructure. Traditional methods of farming predominate, with little support from central government.

As recent events have highlighted, Pakistan is highly susceptible to environmental, political and social catastrophes that reinforce the cycle of poverty. Continual setbacks combined with minimal access to affordable preventative and recuperative healthcare depress the ability of communities to tolerate further problems, and weaken the authority and legitimacy of social, legal and political foundations, which are the basis for stable society.

Environmental Issues

Poor natural resource management over many years and continuing high population growth have had a negative impact on Pakistan's environment. Agricultural runoff caused by ongoing deforestation, and industrial runoff caused by poor infrastructure, have polluted water supplies, while factory and vehicle emissions have degraded air quality in urban centres. In common with other developing countries, Pakistan has sought to achieve self-sufficiency in food production, meet its domestic energy demands, and contain its high rate of population growth, rather than focusing on curtailing pollution and managing other environmental hazards.

A number of serious environmental problems exist, which pose grave ecological concerns for the future, including soil erosion, pesticides misuse, deforestation, desertification, urban pollution, flooding, water salinity, and pollution of freshwater and marine water sources.

The particular demands of water are a pressing concern in Pakistan as they are in other arid regions of the planet. In many areas of the globe water is currently being harvested unsustainably through the tapping of aquifers at unsustainable levels that will deplete these vital and hard-won resources in the coming decades.

> With finite fresh water resources on the one hand, and increasing demand, both in quantity and variety of uses, on the other, the need for water resources protection and management has never been greater. Major clashes over dwindling supplies of water may well constitute the source of future conflicts between nations."[49]

> *(Elizabeth Dowdeswell, United Nations Under-Secretary General and Executive Director, United Nations Environment Programme)*

Freshwater Pollution

Chemical waste:

Most chemical waste is dumped untreated into the river system from where it flows to the sea or discharged into storm-drains. Consequently, it is responsible for many of the water-borne diseases that plague the country and is held to account for 60% of infant deaths. Industrial waste also contaminates the irrigation systems of some vegetable and fruit farms in industrial areas, whose produce shows significantly higher traces of metals and other toxins.

Sewage:

The discharge of sewage and contaminated water in rivers and water bodies affects not only marine life, but also agriculture and consequent contamination of the food chain. Sewage water containing pathogens is re-channelled to irrigate crops, resulting in the contamination of a large percentage of crops in Pakistan.

Agricultural Run-Off and Pesticides:

Water pollution is further exacerbated by agricultural run-off from fields using pesticides and fertilisers, which given the increasing use of agricultural chemicals has already started to affect the purity of underground aquifers.

Marine Pollution

Due to the misconception that the world's oceans are so large they can absorb whatever is spilled into them, they have served as man's dumping grounds for decades. Yet most contaminated water entering the sea has a different density to that of natural seawater, which means the two do not mix and the waste does not dilute effectively. In places it settles down at the bottom of the ocean as sludge, which may be 1.5 feet deep in certain areas. Changes in the density, temperature and chemical make-up of water in the ocean, though seemingly invisible to mankind, can form insuperable barriers to ocean life and become apparent to us only once their effects have become entrenched.

Given the limited understanding of the consequences such actions may have, it is prudent to act in a manner that reflects this and to reassert a concern for, and stewardship of, the planet in the interests of future generations and not selfishly devour it for our own consumption. However, a large number of religious people do focus on environment, as the believe:

> The world is sweet and verdant green, and Allah appoints you to be His regents in it, and will see how you acquit yourselves.
>
> *(Sunnah of the Prophet)*

Domestic sources of marine pollution:

- Industrial effluents

- Waste oil and spillages

- Garbage disposal

- Solid waste

- Metal scrap

- Rust from old shipping

- Oil and liquid waste from fish processing plants

- Spillage of cargoes

- Pollution from passing ships and deck washing

> Plastic bags are found all over the harbour and are not only an eyesore but also damaging to marine life. A wide-diversity of garbage including wood and plastic are also apparent. The garbage originates from the municipal waste and port activities. Water circulation and wind driven currents concentrate this in certain parts of the harbour, making it unsightly and dangerous to ships as it can get stuck in propellers. It can be expected that there is also a significant amount of solid waste, which will have sunk to the bed of the harbour.

> *(Neville Burt, Environmental Assessment and Protection of Karachi Harbour, 1997)*

Forestry

Forests, scrub and planted trees on farmland constitute about 4.2 million hectares (4.8%) of the country.[50] Coniferous varieties and scrub comprise 40% of the total, with irrigated plantations and riverine and coastal forest zones making up the rest. 1.78 million hectares of land is covered by hill forests that include species such as deodar, fir, blue pine, spruce, juniper, chir pine, oak and horse chestnut.[51] These forests grow in the watershed areas protecting the fragile mountain ecosystem, helping to restrict both flooding and drought. As a major source of timber, fuel wood and resin, these forests have come under increasing pressure, which is further exacerbated by escalating demands for grazing land from farmers.

Fuel Wood

Consumption of household firewood exceeds production in all provinces except in the sparsely populated northern areas of Pakistan. An increasing population suggests firewood consumption will rise by 3% per annum and that Pakistan's store of woody biomass may be exhausted within 10 to 15 years.[52]

Soil Erosion

Soil erosion is taking place at an alarming rate, due mainly to deforestation in the north of the country. Around 16 million hectares of land, some 18% of Pakistan's total land area, are affected by soil erosion – 11.2 million hectares by water erosion and 4.8 million hectares by wind erosion.[53]

Water Erosion

Water erosion and poor land management mostly affects watersheds in the upper Indus River and its tributaries, which are extensively used for cultivation. The highest recorded rate of erosion is in the Indus catchment area between the Tarbela reservoir and 90km upstream, where soil loss is estimated to be 150-165 tonnes per hectare per year. Overall, 28% of ground soil is being lost to water erosion, and in the first decade of the Tarbela Dam being completed, 14% of its storage capacity was lost. According to some estimates the Indus adds 500,000 tonnes of sediment to the Tarbela Reservoir every day, reducing the life of the dam by 22% and the capacity of the reservoir by 16%.[54]

Wind Erosion

Wind erosion has a relatively lower impact than water erosion in terms of soil dispersed, but is the more devastating, reducing the productivity of the land by 1.5% to 7.5% per year, and affecting nearly one-fifth of the Punjab.[55]

The Economic Cost

The consequence of environmental degradation and poor resource management is economic loss to Pakistan and her population. The impact of degradation and biodiversity loss on productivity and public health is conservatively estimated at 3% of GDP per annum, which still does not take into consideration the costs of subsequent toxic waste disposal, and river and coastal resource depletion. The health cost of polluted water is estimated at approximately US$750 million p.a. and the cost of air pollution another US$300 million p.a.

Overuse and wastage of water in the agricultural sector have reached a critical stage in Pakistan. After two decades of growth in the sector, loss of water resources combined with erratic precipitation (due to climate change) and water dispersal (due to poor land management) have left the agricultural sector with minimal ability to absorb external shocks and at the same time highly vulnerable to widespread catastrophic events.

The effect of this subsequent insecurity depresses investment in future growth and economic instability from environmental problems increases social and political tensions throughout the country and neighbouring regions. Only once recognition returns amongst all stakeholders that prosperity is built first from the land upwards, can secure and equitable prosperity come to the people of Pakistan.

Photo Gallery Bangladesh & India

In Narayangong 7 years old boy is selling traditional sweets to 70 years old man. This is in the middle of the street and you can also see the Rickshaw.

This is outside the Dhaka Airport in Bangladesh and the boy is happy to carry you suitcases for 20 to 50 pence

*Narayangong High School, one of the oldest schools in Bangladesh;
established in the late 1885s during the British Period. Students are
eating uncovered unhealthy food and this is the picture of future leaders.*

This photo is in Narayangong 15 kilometres away from Dhaka, well-known for garments and other factories. New developments are affecting both soil and water. The location of this photo was farmland 5 to 7 years ago.

*I was providing hands on training to street hawkers regarding
Health Safety and some business techniques (i.e. how to cover food,
how to sell more by showing professionalism and cleanliness).*

*After the rains in Kolkata, rubbish left uncollected
by cleaners mix with overflowing streams*

*Food vendor in Kolkata surrounded by unsanitary
conditions and these are same in Bangladesh*

Roadside vendor in Kolkata selling uncovered food

A STUDY OF GLOBAL ENVIRONMENTAL ISSUES

Managing Changing Ecosystems

An Introduction to Ecosystems

An ecosystem is a biological community that can be local or global in size and aspect. In the second half of the 20th century, the structure of global ecosystems changed more rapidly than at any other time in recorded human history, most significantly the conversion of forests and grasslands to cultivated lands, countryside to urban landscapes, the diversion and storage of freshwater behind dams, and degradation of mangroves and coral reefs.

To human eyes the work of nature can appear invisible. We do not see the chemical processes that enable forests to store carbon or the role of one species in maintaining the food chain. These ecological services are not only invisible but free. Yet while they are free, in economics their existence entails the cost of their maintenance and an opportunity cost amounting to the value of resources which could function in their place. Assigning a value to these services remains problematic for mankind in that we do not have a full understanding of the processes involved within ecosystems, even if assigning a nominal value does seek to recognise the long-term value of such systems.

The Millennium Ecosystem Assessment Synthesis Report notes economists' estimates of these services as being worth at least US$33 trillion per annum, if they were to be undertaken by humans.[56] This is a nominal figure, for many of the services are beyond the ability of mankind to perform. This estimate, moreover, assesses the economic cost of substituting the work of these systems, and not the inherent role of ecosystems as the intended home for humans that is beyond calculation.

Marine, Coastal and Island Ecosystems

The attractiveness of coastal areas have resulted in construction and changing land use patterns that have increased pressures on coastal systems. Coastal systems refer to the interface between ocean and land, extending seawards to about the middle of the continental shelf and inland to include all areas strongly influenced by proximity to the ocean. The development of the tourism sector, recreational hunting and increased demand for food has seen fishing and pollution in coastal areas grow. At the same time, the benefits provided by these increasingly important ecosystems are ignored in conventional economic statistics as resources such as water and biodiversity are not traded in markets. And yet the huge store of water in the world's oceans is essential to the global weather system, while its wealth of species help to support life on Earth and provide a proportion of the raw materials for the pharmaceutical industry.

Meanwhile, until very recently the extent and composition of the world's oceans was unknown and consequently seen as an unbounded natural resource. The weight of recent scientific data has shown how far this is from the truth. Since the emergence of industrial fishing, it is estimated that commercially exploited marine species have seen numbers fall by 90% in much of the world.[57] Fishing stocks in coastal regions have collapsed resulting in the decimation of local fishing industries, while in the vacuum the main beneficiaries have been marine invertebrates such as squid.

According to Nitin Desai, Secretary General of the 2002 World Summit on Sustainable Development, "Overfishing cannot continue, the depletion of fisheries poses a major threat to the food supply of millions of people."[58]

Freshwater Ecosystems

Freshwater sources have been modified by the creation of dams, development of transportation, new city developments and the withdrawal of water for human use, which have changed the flow of many small and large river systems. They also suffer from changing land use elsewhere which have resulted in increased flooding, landslides and droughts.

Where supply and demand have dictated a decease in intensive farming in one region, this is usually made up in increased exports from another region, as can be seen in the fisheries industry where approximately half of all fish exports are from the developing world. Such exports mitigate the collapsed European fish stocks in the Mediterannean and the North Sea.

Forest Ecosystems

Forest systems cover 30% of the Earth's landmass, though this is only half of its size a few centuries ago. Forests have effectively disappeared in 25 countries, while another 29 countries have seen their forests contract by over 90%. Yet forest ecosystems make a significant contribution to carbon storage and are a key link in the water cycle, with approximately 4.6 billion people relying on them as a source of water supply.

Forests systems exist both in temperate and tropical zones. From 1990 to 2000, global cover of temperate forests rose by around 3 million hectares p.a., although some of this is due to commercial replanting of single species less beneficial to the restoration of biodiversity. Meanwhile deforestation in the tropics occurred at an average rate in excess of 12 million hectares p.a. over the last twenty years.[59]

Farmland Ecosystems

Cultivated systems, including croplands, shifting cultivation, confined livestock production and freshwater aquaculture, cover approximately one quarter of the Earth's total land area. As the pressure to satisfy food demand has increased throughout the globe, more than half of the many types of grasslands, forestlands or forests have been converted to farmland, with only tundra and boreal forests having so far escaped with little impact. However even these will come under increasing threat as a result of predicted climate changes in the coming decades.

Technological improvements continue to increase the scope for more productivity gains and in some temperate regions it has already enabled the reconversion of farmland into forests or to be taken out of production to enable the soil to regain fertility.[60]

It has helped to ensure that much of the vast increase in food production over the last half a century has been met through intensification of crop, livestock, and aquaculture systems rather than through the expansion of production areas. In developing countries over the period from 1961 to 1999, expansion of harvested land contributed only 29% to growth in crop production, although there were large disparities from region to region, where in sub-Saharan Africa expansion into new areas accounted for two thirds of production growth.

Mountain Ecosystems

Nearly 1.2 billion people live in mountainous regions or at their fringes, of which 90% are from developing or transition economies. In these countries, 7% of mountainous regions are used for crop and livestock farming, and there is consistent illegal source use as a result of minimal regulation and enforcement.

There are some 4 billion people dependent on mountain systems for some or all of their water supplies, with a similar number benefiting, directly or indirectly, from its mineral resources. Of the 90 million people living in mountainous regions above 2,500 metres, almost all live in poverty and are considered especially vulnerable to food and medicine shortages.[61]

Urban & Dryland Ecosystems

Urban systems are built environments with high human population densities. Over the course of the 20th century, the world's urban population rose from 200 million to 2.9 billion, while the number of cities with over a million inhabitants increased from 17 to 388.

Dryland systems are areas identified by limited water availability, grazing and arable cultivated land, scrublands, grasslands, savannas, semi-deserts, and true deserts. Drylands cover approximately 41% of the planet's land surface and is home to more than 2 billion people.

With almost half the world's population becoming urbanised, urban developments now impose ever-increasing pressures on surrounding and more distant non-urban ecosystems.

Ecosystem Services and Changing Use Patterns

Human use of ecosystem services is growing rapidly and approximately 60% of the ecosystem services evaluated in the Millennium Ecosystem Assessment have been classified as degraded or exploited in an unsustainable manner.[62]

Provisioning Services

Provisioning ecosystem services refer to resources such as food, water, and timber. Their use grew rapidly during the second half of the 20th century, often more rapidly than population growth although generally slower than economic growth. From 1960 to 2000, while the world population doubled and the global economy grew more than six fold, food production increased by two-and-a-half times.

Regulating Services

These are the benefits that result from the regulation of ecosystem processes, for example the regulation of air quality. All ecosystems involve a complex interplay of chemical and biological materials that in certain configurations and quantities are toxic or detrimental to surrounding life. Changes in land use can affect local climates and beyond. Instability in the El Nino cycle or the high temperatures experienced across Russia in the summer of 2010 were both a consequence of ecosystem changes originating half a world away.

Humans have substantially altered regulating services such as disease and climate by modifying ecosystems providing the service and, in the case of waste processing services, by exceeding the capabilities of ecosystems tasked with their biodegradation. Most changes to regulating services are the inadvertent results of actions taken to enhance the supply of provisioning services. Humans have substantially modified the climate regulation service of ecosystems - first through land use changes that contributed to increases in the amount of carbon dioxide and other greenhouse gases such as methane and nitrous oxide expelled into the atmosphere and more recently by increased sequestration of carbon dioxide, though ecosystems remain a net source of methane and nitrous oxide. Ecosystems can be a source of impurities but can also help filter out and decompose organic wastes introduced into inland waters and coastal and marine ecosystems, and can assimilate and detoxify compounds through soil and subsoil processes. Changes in ecosystems can directly change the abundance of human pathogens, such as cholera, and can alter the abundance of disease carriers, such as the mosquito. They have also affected the distribution, abundance, and effectiveness of pollinators.

The Effects of Ecosystem Changes on Human Well-Being and Poverty Alleviation

Living standards have their foundations in material welfare, good health, good social relations, quality of food supply, availability of fresh water, safety and freedom of action. All of these are directly or indirectly affected by changes in the supply of ecosystem services, which can suffer exponentially in reply to shortages.

Poorer populations are less insulated from supply shortages than their wealthier counterparts, lacking reserves of individual or collective resources, and reliant on undeveloped and inefficient institutions. Poverty tends to increase pressure on ecosystem services and can lead to a downward spiral of poverty and ecosystem degradation. The effects are nevertheless felt by wealthier populations also, as can be seen presently in an indirect fashion through waves of immigration from impoverished regions to Europe and the United States of America.

Intensive ecosystem use produces short-term benefits, but excessive and sustained exploitation can result in greater long-term costs. Cutting forests for timber and depleting fish stocks for export will register an immediate positive gain in GDP, but what is not recorded is the loss of future earnings potential and environmental consequences. The accepted practice should be that which exists in all responsible corporate boardrooms, where utilisation of the fruits of the production process stands alongside the protection of capital assets. Where capital assets are depleted, this should be under recourse to a long-term plan that envisages the short-term gains not for consumption, but as an investment that will lead to an increase in capital assets in the long-term. An example could be the construction of schools and medical facilities that will lead to a more knowledgeable and healthy society, which can subsequently use its technical expertise and vitality to maintain a balanced and prosperous lifestyle.

Consideration must be given to the ownership and the distribution of ecosystem resources. There have been large strides in improving agricultural productivity in South Asia, but has there been a corresponding improvement in the welfare of those working the fields? If so, why do so many remain impoverished and opt to migrate to the cities?

A Summary of Factors behind Changing Ecosystems

Demographic Factors

The unprecedented expansion of the human population in terms of rates and numbers has placed enormous strain on the planet's resources. It has been accompanied by lifestyle changes that have significantly increased the short-term and long-term environmental footprint of each individual.

Cultural and Religious Factors

Culture conditions individuals' perceptions of the world, it influences what they consider important, and it suggests what courses of action are appropriate and inappropriate. Broad comparisons of whole cultures have not proved useful because they ignore vast variations in values, beliefs, and norms within cultures. Nevertheless, cultural differences influence patterns in consumption behavior, specific values related to environmental stewardship, and may be particularly important drivers of environmental change.

Economic Factors

Global economic activity has increased nearly seven-fold in the last 50 years, with per capita growth signalling an increase in consumption, in particular, of industrially manufactured produce. This production process is energy intensive, reliant on chemical compositions that are toxic in concentration, inefficient when comparing inputs versus outputs, and culpable in the production of high volumes of non-biodegadable waste.

Taxes and subsidies are becoming an increasingly important tool in shifting towards more sustainable economies, to changing the emphasis to new technology sectors, to incentivise a more efficient use of fossil fuels and, more contentiously, eventually to target consumption itself. Nevertheless the situation is haphazard. Subsidies for conventional energy sit alongside those for renewable energy, while initiatives to protect natural habitats sit alongside agricultural subsidies that encourage oversupply.[63]

Sociopolitical Factors

These encompass the forces influencing decision-making, which in turn affect insitutional arrangements for ecosystem management, property rights over ecosystem services and enforcement of legislation.

Recent decades have seen a decline of centralised authoritarian governments and a consequent rise in elected democracies. Sometimes this has translated to increased public participation in decision-making, but it does not simply equate to increased power for local communities, as power has also shifted to other bodies such as corporate boardrooms and unaccountable public institutions.

Increased participation of women, the influence of state education, and mechanisms for dispute resolution have all brought changes in dealing with these issues, though it would not be possible to say that these have resulted in uniformly positive or negative implications for ecosystems.

Science and Technological Factors

Technological changes are a driving force not only behind economic growth, but also public attitudes, culture and human communication. Technology is the single most transformative factor in human society and the reason for increasing human supremacy. While the power that humans yield has increased, our control over this power has not kept pace. Humans still remain susceptible to natural factors on the large scale and the small scale. At the same time, human specialisation, which has resulted as a response to meet the demands of an increasingly technological economy, and declining inherited land-based knowledge, leave humans further susceptible to environmental changes.

The driving forces behind environmental change are often many and dynamic. For this reason human intervention in protecting the environment has to proceed with caution, as we do not yet fully comprehend what will be the full consequences of our actions. It is nevertheless prudent to assume that, while the environment is always undergoing a process of change, it is our duty to minimise some of the excessive transformations which human activity has in recent decades imposed on fragile and carefully balanced ecosystems.

Scenarios for Future Ecosystem Changes

The Millennium Ecosystem Assessment,[64] developed by the World Resources Institute, UNEP, UNDP and World Bank, outlined four plausible global scenarios for 2050 based upon whether the approach to problems was dealt with on a global or fragmented/regional basis, and whether actions were taken proactively or reactively.

Global Orchestration

Global approach, undertaken reactively

- Based around global trade and economic liberalisation, with steps taken to reduce poverty and inequality, and greater investment in human and material infrastructure.

- Predicts the highest economic growth and lowest population growth of the four scenarios by 2050.

Order from Strength

Fragmented approach, undertaken reactively

- Based around regional trade, with fewer steps taken to address inequalities, ecosystem changes and investment in public goods.

- Predicts the lowest economic growth and highest population growth (especially in the poorest nations) of the four scenarios by 2050.

Adapting Mosaic

Regional approach, undertaken proactively

- A focus on co-ordinated regional ecosystem management,

supported by strong local institutions and civil society in a proactive manner.

- Predicts improving economic growth after a slow start and the second-highest population growth of the four scenarios by 2050.

Techno Garden

Global approach, undertaken proactively

- Based around global trade supported by environmentally-friendly technology, working towards highly managed and engineered ecosystems and ecosystem service delivery.

- Predicts relatively high and accelerating economic growth, and medium population growth by 2050.

The scenarios above present simplified strategies. In the real world, strategies will likely present a mix of all the above approaches and perhaps alternatives not yet foreseen. They do nevertheless present an analysis of the broad paths to be considered by today's policymakers and stakeholders, the idealised vision one might say which they will strive to achieve, and the opportunity to consider costs and benefits of each. A localised approach could result in lower growth and lower transfer of technological solutions, but could also prevent migrations of potential harmful species and diseases. It is trade-offs such as these, which reflect the complex decision-making faced by current and future generations as they engage in these issues from within increasingly globalised human societies and pressurised ecosystems.

The Consequences of Future Ecosystem Changes on Human Well-Being and Poverty Alleviation

All four of the scenarios above envisage increasing human use of ecosystem services, in many cases accompanied by degradation of the quality of service available, and where exploited unsustainably, in the quantity also.

Demand for food crops is projected to grow by 70% to 85% by 2050 and global water extraction by 20% to 85% across all scenarios. Water withdrawals are projected to increase significantly in developing countries but to decline in OECD countries. The quantity and quality of ecosystem services will change dramatically during this time as productivity of some services is increased to meet demand, as humans use a greater fraction of some services, and as some services are diminished or degraded. Ecosystem services that are projected to be further impaired by ecosystem change include fisheries and food production in drylands, and could result in less diversified diets in poor countries.[65]

Food insecurity will remain a fact of life for many people and child malnutrition is projected to increase in some regions under some scenarios, in spite of increased food supply under all four scenarios. The combination of low current levels of human well-being (high rates of poverty, low per capita GDP, high infant mortality rates), a large and growing population, high variability of environmental conditions in dryland regions, and the high sensitivity of people to changes in ecosystem services will result in continued land degradation that could have profoundly negative further impacts on the well-being of large numbers of people in these regions.[66]

Timescale and Inertia in Ecosystem Changes

Much of the impact of human activity on ecosystems can be slow to become apparent, and this can result in the costs associated with ecosystem changes being deferred to future generations. The exploitation of underground aquifers, which have taken millions of years to store up but are depleted over decades, is a typical example. The full understanding of the scale and effects of this depletion have only recently become apparent.

As ecosystem resources tend to be communally owned, the incentives for individuals to maximise their share of the resource in the short-term outweigh the incentives to protect the resource for others, both for the present and for the future. Another view of the situation is that individual logic will seek to maximise the fully graspable benefits in the short-term and ignore predictions of long-term costs as these are uncertain, involve a far greater degree of complexity and caveats, and given the often apocalyptic scenarios envisaged, are difficult to comprehend.

The inevitable short-term incentives that affect individuals, also affect business leaders and politicians.

When one looks at the loss of biodiversity, the source is often habitat destruction with causes that stretch across the globe. The loss of habitat of orangutans in Sumatra is a result of the trade in hardwoods such as mahogany, ebony and sandalwood fed by demand in Europe, America and Asia, as well as a result of the conversion of land for palm oil plantations which feed a product that is an ingredient in a surprisingly high proportion of the goods consumed across the world. For many smaller species, as with those suffering loss of habitat due to the destruction of the Amazonian rainforest as a result of the global demand for beef, the process of extinction may take decades and may even, like many extinctions, go unnoticed by mankind.

While habitat loss can lead to rapid extinction of some species especially those with limited geographical ranges, for many species extinction will only occur after several generations, and long-lived species such as some trees could persist for centuries before ultimately going extinct.

Non-Linear Changes in Ecosystems

Most of the time, change in ecosystems and their services is gradual and incremental. Non-linear changes, on the other hand, refer to accelerating, abrupt, and potentially irreversible transformations that usually occur when particular pressure on an ecosystem reaches a threshold. At this point changes occur relatively rapidly and can become a self-perpetuating and self-accelerating cycle.

One such self-perpetuating example comes from mechanisms affected by the onset of global warming, where melting ice sheets and snow areas release greenhouse gases into the atmosphere that have been trapped for millennia, further accelerating global warming. Rising temperatures simultaneously lead to increased levels of water vapour that magnify the effect of greenhouse gases.

The capabilities for predicting certain non-linear changes are improving, but remain at a primitive level, particularly in predicting the actual thresholds when non-linear change will be encountered.

Potential for Sustainable Ecosystem Management

While the degradation of ecosystems presents major challenges, the

Millennium Ecosystem Assessment scenarios show these can be met if the necessary changes to outlook, policies, institutions and engagement are implemented to mitigate the effects of increased demand on ecosystem services, to maximise the scale and spread of future efficiency savings, and to manage consumption patterns.

To highlight the disparity between where we currently are and where we could be under the Millennium Ecosystem Assessment scenarios:

- In the Global Orchestration scenario, trade barriers are eliminated, inefficient and wasteful subsidies are removed, and a major emphasis is placed on eliminating poverty and hunger.

- In the Adapting Mosaic scenario, by 2010 most countries are spending close to 13% of GDP on education (compared with an average of 3.5% in 2000), and institutional arrangements exist to promote the transfer of skills and knowledge among regional groups.

- In the Techno Garden scenario, policies are instituted that financially reward individuals and companies that maintain ecosystem services. For example, in this scenario, by 2015 roughly 50% of European agriculture and 10% of North American agriculture is aimed at balancing the production of food with the production of other ecosystem services. Significant advances are envisaged in the development of environmental technologies, although important gaps in the distribution of protected areas remain, particularly in marine and freshwater systems.

The Decision-Making Process in Ecosystem Management

Decisions affecting ecosystems and their services can be improved by changing the processes used to reach those decisions. Decisions are not made in an objective vacuum, but reflect the interests, conceptions, knowledge and sympathies of those making the decisions, as well as the influences, pressures, scrutiny and accountability they face. The Millennium Ecosystem Assessment identifies the following elements that tend to improve decision-making and their outcomes for ecosystems and human well-being:

- Use of the best available information, including considerations of the value of both marketed and non-marketed ecosystem services.

- Transparency and the effective and informed participation of important stakeholders.

- Recognition that not all values at stake can be quantified, and that quantification can be a false objectivity in decision processes that entail significant subjective judgments.

- An emphasis on efficiency, but not at the expense of effectiveness.

- Consideration of equity and vulnerability in the distribution of costs and benefits.

- Appropriate institutional and governance arrangements supported by strong regulatory and accountability systems throughout the entire decision-making process and subsequent implementation process.

- Consideration of implications across different ecosystem services.

- Astute alignment of economic incentives and market forces.

Given the wide array of factors affecting and affected by ecosystem changes, and the need to accommodate local and global interests, it is prudent that decisions are informed by the participation of stakeholders who represent the wide range of interests and knowledge relevant to the matter at hand. This not only increases the likelihood of reaching the wisest and most equitable decisions, but also the subsequent legitimacy of decisions and their long-term efficient implementation.

Changes in institutional and environmental governance frameworks are sometimes required in order to create the enabling conditions for effective management of ecosystems, while in other cases existing institutions could meet these needs but face significant barriers. Many existing institutions at both the global and the national level have the mandate to address the degradation of ecosystem services but face a variety of challenges in doing so related to the need for greater co-operation across sectors and the need for co-ordinated responses on different levels.

Issues of ownership and access to resources, rights to participation in decision-making, and regulation of particular types of resource use or discharge of wastes can strongly influence the sustainability of ecosystem management and are fundamental determinants of who wins and who loses from changes in ecosystems. Corruption, a major obstacle to effective management of ecosystems, also stems from weak systems of regulation and accountability.

The most important public policy decisions affecting ecosystems are often made by agencies and in policy arenas other than those charged with protecting ecosystems. Ecosystem management goals are more likely to be achieved if they are reflected in decisions in other sectors and in national development strategies. For example, the Poverty Reduction Strategies prepared by developing-country governments for the World Bank and other institutions strongly shape national development priorities, but in general these have not taken into account the importance of ecosystems to improving the basic human capabilities of the poorest.[67]

Towards Sustainable Energy

Introduction

Energy is present in many forms - its immediate creative power is familiarly experienced by us through heat, light, electricity, and nuclear and chemical reactions - but it can also be identified in two groups, those that are from renewable sources and those from non-renewable sources.

Renewable energy sources are those that can be replenished naturally in a short time period (in other words, where replenishment is at least equal to consumption) and can be considered to include solar, biomass, wind, tidal, geothermal and hydro energy. Non-renewable energy sources are those whose replenishment cannot keep up with their depletion. Non-renewable sources are extracted from the ground as liquids, gases and solids, typically having taken millennia to accumulate. Coal, petroleum, natural gas, and propane are all considered fossil fuels, which formed from the buried remains of plants and animals millions of years ago. [68]

The efficient use of energy is fundamental to achieving sustainable development goals, as it is part of a delicate balance, for while it enables socio-economic development it also contributes to degradation of the environment's resources. It is one of defining challenges of 21st century for while the demand for energy is soaring as never before, we often forget to ask where will this energy come from? This is a burning question for us, which we, as corporations, governments, policymakers, scientists and global citizens face together.

At present, across the globe 1.6 billion people lack access to electricity and 2.4 billion people rely on traditional biomass for their cooking and heating needs. Inadequate supply of energy and access to energy services contributes to poverty and impedes efforts towards sustainable development and to achieving all of the Millennium Development Goals. The criterion for energy use is that it is efficient and responsible. In 2002, the World Summit on Sustainable Development identified clearly established links between energy reduction and poverty reduction, resulting in the need to address unsustainable patterns of consumption and production.

Background Analysis

In this Handbook, we have to justify issues such as sustainable energy consumption or production. At present, energy consumption is the ultimate cause of the challenges faced by energy supply and energy policies.

Transportation is responsible for a quarter of human greenhouse gas emissions, with burning of fossil fuels accounting for 75% to 85% of global carbon dioxide emissions. Deforestation and other land use changes mainly in tropical countries account for the rest.

If we look around the world, trends in global energy use appear uniformly unsustainable given present technological capabilities. Oil demand continues to grow, while experts expect a historic peak in oil production by the next 20 years. Carbon dioxide emissions from fossil fuel combustion in 2002 were about 13% above the 1990 levels, whereas a stabilisation of climate trends would require a 50% reduction by 2050 and further reductions thereafter. For OECD countries this would require reduction targets of between 60% to 80% in order to allow developing countries a temporary increase in emissions.

The world's richest people, earning over US$20,000 per annum, consume nearly twenty-five times as much energy per person as the poorest. Nearly one third of the world's population have no access to electricity and another third only poor access, yet their environmental impact is significant given their reliance on traditional fuels for cooking and heating which have a serious impact on health and the environment.

Consuming energy is a means to an end, that end being the provision of needs and wants for cooking, lighting, heating, mobility and production of goods. What are needs and what are wants varies from generation to generation and region to region. Essentially, needs and wants become relative, and it is for us as stakeholders to determine the appropriate climate in which such decisions are made.

The challenge for sustainable energy consumption and production is, therefore, to satisfy the appropriate level of energy-related needs of every human being. From there, the big question is how can energy use be made more sustainable? The answer to this question is one that will vary in different parts of the world.

The Intergovernmental Panel on Climate Change warns that failure to act now to reduce greenhouse gas emissions will lead to costly risks to society, the economy and the planet. These risks include shortages of water and extensive drought, more extreme weather events, lower yields from agriculture in already vulnerable areas, a reduction in biodiversity, and increased susceptibility to diseases. And it is, and will continue to be, the poorer countries that will suffer disproportionately, being most vulnerable to the effects of climate change and least able to ameliorate its effects.

Sustainable Energy Sources

The renewable energy sources with most significant potential are biofuels, solar power, wind power, wave power, tidal power and geothermal power. The use of such sources must be combined with technologies to increase energy efficiency and mitigate the harmful effects of energy use, as well as consistent efforts to reduce consumption and engineer more energy efficient lifestyles.

Biomass / Biofuels

Biofuels are seen as environmentally-friendly alternatives to fossil fuels, with the potential also to reduce over-centralisation of energy supply networks. A UN report identifies biomass for combined heat and power, rather than for transport fuels or other uses, as the best and cheapest way to reduce greenhouse gas emissions over the next decade. It also proposes the use of liquid biofuels for transportation to accompany reductions in vehicle use and car size.

Biofuels are carbon neutral and global production of energy crops is doubling every few years, with 17 countries so far having committed themselves to growing the crops on a large scale. These crops have the potential to reduce and stabilise the price of oil, which would be beneficial for poorer countries. But the United Nations acknowledges that forests are already being felled to provide the land to grow vast plantations of palm oil trees. This can be catastrophic for the climate as the loss of forests reduces the future carbon storage capacity of the Earth and releases stored up carbon into the atmosphere in the short-term. It also reduces the planet's biodiversity, as tropical rainforests such as the Amazon, which is at the forefront of this particular land use issue, are by a long way the most biodiverse regions on Earth.

Solar Power

Solar cell technologies can provide electrical generation through heat or photovoltaic means and have the benefit of being relatively unobtrusive as a means of energy production. Its adaptability to small-scale and mobile applications enables it support a wide range of applications, from industrial processes to water purification in isolated areas.

Wind Power

This ancient form of energy production has been propelled into the 21st century by technological advances which have enabled the building of turbines with sufficient power generation capability to make it a sensible option to meet present-day energy consumption needs. While sometimes considered visually obtrusive, it can be adapted to small-scale generation for small communities and it makes use of a widely distributed and plentiful natural feature.

Wave Power

The energy contained within waves around the world is immense and offers the opportunity for large generating stations to be built to supply energy needs. It is a direct and clean means to convert the energy of waves and has a particularly strong potential application for small island states such as the Maldives and Sri Lanka, or countries with large coastal regions.

Tidal Power

Tidal energy is produced through the use of tidal energy generators by placing large underwater turbines in areas with high tidal movements to capture the kinetic motion of the ebbing and surging of ocean tides. Though still in its infancy, tidal energy has the potential to deliver energy more efficiently than wind turbines, given the higher density of water to air.

Geothermal Power

Geothermal power is energy generated from heat stored underground, or the collection of absorbed heat derived from below ground, the atmosphere and the oceans. While it is a form of extraction, the amount is minimal compared with the nearly inexhaustible supply of energy stored within the Earth. It also benefits from relative immunity to changes in weather conditions.

CONCLUSIONS

Summary

For more than 50 years, the World Bank, donor governments, aid agencies and non-governmental organisations have tried their best to engineer a profound change in global development efforts, but the general situation for many of the intended beneficiaries has changed little.

Due to the complex web of the global ecosystem, the consequences of an increase in global temperatures will vary from place to place, but according to the United Nations' Intergovernmental Panel on Climate Change, the most authoritative source on global warming, changes will include rising sea levels of up to three feet by 2100, an increase in extreme weather events, a loss of biodiversity, decreasing crop yields, increasing water scarcity and the spread of infectious diseases.

Issues of governance, responsibility and accountability are becoming increasing important as the urgency for the world to unite to confront these issues becomes more transparent. These issues are further heightened by the increasing dominance of corporations within a globalised network of media attention and internet-led democracy. As a result, this Handbook has sought to unite discussion of these prevailing circumstances in the South Asian arena.

Business and Sustainable Development

Business provides the economic vehicle for development, for nations as well as individuals. The business sector is, in other words, essential to the development and protection of human rights for over 6 billion people on this planet, and without sustainable development, fundamental human rights cannot be secured. Far from being in conflict, business and sustainable development are dependent upon one another.

Many socially responsible companies view human rights issues as a fundamental part of their business environment – they refuse to separate corporate responsibility from their own personal responsibility, they refuse to say that their actions in business bear no reflection on their own character and morality. Many such business leaders are setting their own standards for openness and for their dealings with other stakeholders. But these remain a minority and there will always remain a need for society's scrutiny of corporate activity, with good practice rewarded and bad practice penalised.

Moving Forward

We have discussed and analysed many issues related to energy consumption, sustainable development and climate change. Now in summery I have two questions to pose:

- Who should we blame for the unsustainable and environmentally damaging activities?

- Who should be the caretaker of nature?

Both of these questions have same answer. It is *we*; every single citizen on this globe who should feel responsible and liable for these activities. Of course there are people who act with full consideration of their behaviour and act accordingly. But in many cases we do not know the full extent of our own environmentally unfriendly activities. When the production process is stretched across regions and nations it is easy to forget the processes involved in our end consumption. Similarly it is easy to see the consumption of others and desire the same.

For us all to become caretakers of nature requires a new social compact, similar to the compact that is implicit in each democratic state. An effective global strategy of sustainable development must be based on a policy of sustainable energy and requires a combination of information, practical guidance, regulation, and financial incentives. It will require a complex interplay of undertakings which is possible if the same effort is given to it as to the plethora of short-term profit-making and financial ventures that is the current foundation of the global economy.

As an example, biofuels promise major benefits for livelihoods and the environment, but there can be serious consequences if forests are razed for plantations, or if food prices rise, or communities are excluded from ownership. Unless new policies are enacted to protect threatened lands, secure socially acceptable land use, and steer bioenergy development in a sustainable direction overall, the environmental and social damage could in some cases outweigh the benefits.

Conclusion

It is essential that global leaders be responsive in enabling sustainable trade in its full aspects when configuring our geo-political world. In a report entitled *A Fair Globalization*, the World Commission on the Social Dimension of Globalization states,

> ... Our experience has demonstrated the value and power of dialogue as an instrument for change ... We were spurred on by the realization that action to build a fair and inclusive process of globalization was urgent. This could only happen in the future through forging agreements amongst a broad spectrum of actors on the course for action. We are convinced that our experience can and should be replicated on a larger and wider scale.[69]

The Co-Chairs of the report, Tarja Halonen, President of the Republic of Finland, and Benjamin William Mkapa, President of the United Republic of Tanzania have added that,

> This is an ambitious but realizable common sense vision. The choice is clear. We can correct the global governance deficit in the world today, ensure accountability and adopt coherent policies that forge a path for globalization that is fair and just, both within and between countries, or we can prevaricate and risk a slide into further spirals of insecurity, political turbulence, conflicts and wars.[70]

The United Nations Environment Programme has stated that underpinning all sustainable development initiatives are environmental, economic and socio-political considerations. Furthermore the author of this Handbook asserts that sustainable use of natural resources is key to all economic development. Without a sustainable environment there can be no sustainable development.

But while political leaders help frame the playing field, we all have the ability, incentive and responsibility to affect the rules of the game through our own actions. It is therefore essential for all stakeholders to implement new policies, new thinking and new ways of doing business with sustainable energy consumption in mind. The success of implementing the commitments of the global agenda for sustainable development fully depends upon all stakeholders' active involvement and adoption of ethical practices. Hence this Handbook's strong recommendation to the individuals, governments, business people and policymakers to undertake initiatives and implement legislative strategies addressing sustainable development as a global strategy in order to protect the planet for future generations.

Appendix I: Rio Declaration on Environment and Development [71]

Principle 1

Human beings are at the centre of concerns for sustainable development. They are entitled to a healthy and productive life in harmony with nature.

Principle 2

States have, in accordance with the Charter of the United Nations and the principles of international law, the sovereign right to exploit their own resources pursuant to their own environmental and developmental policies, and the responsibility to ensure that activities within their jurisdiction or control do not cause damage to the environment of other States or of areas beyond the limits of national jurisdiction.

Principle 3

The right to development must be fulfilled so as to equitably meet developmental and environmental needs of present and future generations.

Principle 4

In order to achieve sustainable development, environmental protection shall constitute an integral part of the development process and cannot be considered in isolation from it.

Principle 5

All States and all people shall cooperate in the essential task of eradicating poverty as an indispensable requirement for sustainable development, in order to decrease the disparities in standards of living and better meet the needs of the majority of the people of the world.

Principle 6

The special situation and needs of developing countries, particularly the least developed and those most environmentally vulnerable, shall be given special priority. International actions in the field of environment and development should also address the interests and needs of all countries.

Principle 7

States shall cooperate in a spirit of global partnership to conserve, protect and restore the health and integrity of the Earth's ecosystem. In view of the different contributions to global environmental degradation, States have common but differentiated responsibilities. The developed countries acknowledge the responsibility that they bear in the international pursuit to sustainable development in view of the pressures their societies place on the global environment and of the technologies and financial resources they command.

Principle 8

To achieve sustainable development and a higher quality of life for all people, States should reduce and eliminate unsustainable patterns of production and consumption and promote appropriate demographic policies.

Principle 9

States should cooperate to strengthen endogenous capacity-building for sustainable development by improving scientific understanding through exchanges of scientific and technological knowledge, and by enhancing the development, adaptation, diffusion and transfer of technologies, including new and innovative technologies.

Principle 10

Environmental issues are best handled with participation of all concerned citizens, at the relevant level. At the national level, each individual shall have appropriate access to information concerning the environment that is held by public authorities, including information on hazardous materials and activities in their communities, and the opportunity to participate in decision-making processes. States shall facilitate and encourage public awareness and participation by making information widely available. Effective access to judicial and administrative proceedings, including redress and remedy, shall be provided.

Principle 11

States shall enact effective environmental legislation. Environmental standards, management objectives and priorities should reflect the environmental and development context to which they apply. Standards applied by some countries may be inappropriate and of unwarranted economic and social cost to other countries, in particular developing countries.

Principle 12

States should cooperate to promote a supportive and open international economic system that would lead to economic growth and sustainable development in all countries, to better address the problems of environmental degradation. Trade policy measures for environmental purposes should not constitute a means of arbitrary or unjustifiable discrimination or a disguised restriction on international trade. Unilateral actions to deal with environmental challenges outside the jurisdiction of the importing country should be avoided. Environmental measures addressing transboundary or global environmental problems should, as far as possible, be based on an international consensus.

Principle 13

States shall develop national law regarding liability and compensation for the victims of pollution and other environmental damage. States shall also cooperate in an expeditious and more determined manner to develop further international law regarding liability and compensation for adverse effects of environmental damage caused by activities within their jurisdiction or control to areas beyond their jurisdiction.

Principle 14

States should effectively cooperate to discourage or prevent the relocation and transfer to other States of any activities and substances that cause severe environmental degradation or are found to be harmful to human health.

Principle 15

In order to protect the environment, the precautionary approach shall be widely applied by States according to their capabilities. Where there are threats of serious or irreversible damage, lack of full scientific certainty shall not be used as a reason for postponing cost-effective measures to prevent environmental degradation.

Principle 16

National authorities should endeavour to promote the internalisation of environmental costs and the use of economic instruments, taking into account the approach that the polluter should, in principle, bear the cost of pollution, with due regard to the public interest and without distorting international trade and investment.

Principle 17

Environmental impact assessment, as a national instrument, shall be undertaken for proposed activities that are likely to have a significant adverse impact on the environment and are subject to a decision of a competent national authority.

Principle 18

States shall immediately notify other States of any natural disasters or other emergencies that are likely to produce sudden harmful effects on the environment of those States. Every effort shall be made by the international community to help States so afflicted.

Principle 19

States shall provide prior and timely notification and relevant information to potentially affected States on activities that may have a significant adverse transboundary environmental effect and shall consult with those States at an early stage and in good faith.

Principle 20

Women have a vital role in environmental management and development. Their full participation is therefore essential to achieve sustainable development.

Principle 21

The creativity, ideals and courage of the youth of the world should be mobilized to forge a global partnership in order to achieve sustainable development and ensure a better future for all.

Principle 22

Indigenous people and their communities and other local communities have a vital role in environmental management and development because of their knowledge and traditional practices. States should recognize and duly support their identity, culture and interests and enable their effective participation in the achievement of sustainable development.

Principle 23

The environment and natural resources of people under oppression, domination and occupation shall be protected.

Principle 24

Warfare is inherently destructive of sustainable development. States shall therefore respect international law providing protection for the environment in times of armed conflict and cooperate in its further development, as necessary.

Principle 25

Peace, development and environmental protection are interdependent and indivisible.

Principle 26

States shall resolve all their environmental disputes peacefully and by appropriate means in accordance with the Charter of the United Nations.

Principle 27

States and people shall cooperate in good faith and in a spirit of partnership in the fulfilment of the principles embodied in this Declaration and in the further development of international law in the field of sustainable development.

Appendix II: Objectives of the Convention on Biological Diversity

The objectives of this Convention, to be pursued in accordance with its relevant provisions, are the conservation of biological diversity, the sustainable use of its components and the fair and equitable sharing of the benefits arising out of the utilisation of genetic resources, including by appropriate access to genetic resources and by appropriate transfer of relevant technologies, taking into account all rights over those resources and to technologies, and by appropriate funding.

Appendix III: Statement of Principles for Forest Management

Preamble to the non-legally binding statement of principles for a global consensus on the management, conservation, and sustainable development of all types of forests, adopted at United Nations Conference on Environment and Development, Rio de Janeiro, Brazil, June 13, 1992.

(a) The subject of forests is related to the entire range of environmental and development issues and opportunities, including the right to socio-economic development on a sustainable basis.

(b) The guiding objective of these principles is to contribute to the management, conservation and sustainable development of forests and to provide for their multiple and complementary functions and uses.

(c) Forestry issues and opportunities should be examined in a holistic and balanced manner within the overall context of environment and development, taking into consideration the multiple functions and uses of forests, including traditional uses, and the likely economic and social stress when these uses are constrained or restricted, as well as the potential for development that sustainable forest management can offer.

(d) These principles reflect a first global consensus on forests. In committing themselves to the prompt implementation of these principles, countries also decide to keep them under assessment for their adequacy with regard to further international cooperation on forest issues.

(e) These principles should apply to all types of forests, both natural and planted, in all geographic regions and climatic zones, including austral, boreal, subtemperate, temperate, subtropical and tropical.

(f) All types of forests embody complex and unique ecological processes which are the basis for their present and potential capacity to provide resources to satisfy human needs as well as environmental values, and as such their sound management and conservation is of concern to the Governments of the countries to which they belong and are of value to local communities and to the environment as a whole.

Appendix IV: Oil in Numbers

Crude oil is a finite natural resource extracted from the earth and refined to create a range of gas (LPG), liquid (gasoline, diesel, aviation fuel, paraffin) and solid (bitumen) petroleum products.

According to the Statistical Energy Survey by BP in 2008, the world had proven oil reserves of 1,237.875 billion barrels by the end of 2007, while consuming an average of 85,219.7 thousand barrels a day of oil in 2007. OPEC members hold around 75% of world crude oil reserves. The countries with the largest oil reserves are, in order of quantity, Saudi Arabia, Iran, Iraq, Kuwait, the United Arab Emirates, Venezuela, Russia, Libya, Kazakhstan and Nigeria. The survey also showed that the world had proven natural gas reserves of 177.35 trillion cubic metres and natural gas production of 2,939.99 billion cubic metres in 2007.[72]

On the other hand, the appetite for oil and other energy sources is growing dramatically across the globe, with energy consumption projected to rise more than 50% by 2030. The growing demand is fuelled in countries with emerging economies, such as China, India and Brazil. Rising energy demand from economic output, development of technologies and improved lifestyles will create extra pressure on energy production and supplies, as for example in China where projections estimate more than 100 million new vehicles will be purchased before 2020. Moreover, citizens in the developed world continue to increase energy usage and product consumption.

In 2007 global demand for oil reached 85.7 mbpd, which was 1% up on the 84.9 mbpd consumed in 2006. The major oil consuming nations were, in order of consumption, the USA, China, Japan, Russia, Germany, India, South Korea, Canada, Brazil and Saudi Arabia. China and India accounted for some 70% of the increase in oil demand during 2006 and 2007, with oil producing countries responsible for much of the balance. Between 1996 and 2006, US domestic production fell from 45% to 33% of domestic demand, with net imports larger than the combined production of Saudi Arabia and Kuwait. The US government launched its 20 in 10 initiative to reduce gasoline demand by 20% in 10 years, through improved engine emission standards and the use of ethanol. The IEA forecasts that demand for oil will increase by 10 mbpd to 94.8 mbpd in 2015, with the demand for OPEC oil forecast to increase from the current 31 mbpd to 38.8 mbpd in 2015.[73]

Appendix V: International Labour Organization Conventions

The official conventions adopted by the International Labour Conference:

1. Hours of Work (Industry) Convention, 1919

2. Unemployment Convention, 1919

3. Maternity Protection Convention, 1919

4. Night Work (Women) Convention, 1919 (shelved)

5. Minimum Age (Industry) Convention, 1919

6. Night Work of Young Persons (Industry) Convention, 1919

7. Minimum Age (Sea) Convention, 1920

8. Unemployment Indemnity (Shipwreck) Convention, 1920

9. Placing of Seamen Convention, 1920

10. Minimum Age (Agriculture) Convention, 1921

11. Right of Association (Agriculture) Convention, 1921

12. Workmen's Compensation (Agriculture) Convention, 1921

13. White Lead (Painting) Convention, 1921

14. Weekly Rest (Industry) Convention, 1921

15. Minimum Age (Trimmers and Stokers) Convention, 1921 (shelved)

16. Medical Examination of Young Persons (Sea) Convention, 1921

17. Workmen's Compensation (Accidents) Convention, 1925

18. Workmen's Compensation (Occupational Diseases) Convention, 1925

19. Equality of Treatment (Accident Compensation) Convention, 1925

20. Night Work (Bakeries) Convention, 1925 (shelved)

21. Inspection of Emigrants Convention, 1926 (shelved)

22. Seamen's Articles of Agreement Convention, 1926

23. Repatriation of Seamen Convention, 1926

24. Sickness Insurance (Industry) Convention, 1927

25. Sickness Insurance (Agriculture) Convention, 1927

26. Minimum Wage-Fixing Machinery Convention, 1928

27. Marking of Weight (Packages Transported by Vessels) Convention, 1929

28. Protection against Accidents (Dockers) Convention, 1929 (shelved)

29. Forced Labour Convention, 1930

30. Hours of Work (Commerce and Offices) Convention, 1930

31. Hours of Work (Coal Mines) Convention, 1931 (withdrawn by the ILC – decision of 15 June 2000)

32. Protection against Accidents (Dockers) Convention (Revised), 1932

33. Minimum Age (Non-Industrial Employment) Convention, 1932

34. Fee-Charging Employment Agencies Convention, 1933 (shelved)

35. Old-Age Insurance (Industry, etc.) Convention, 1933 (shelved)

36. Old-Age Insurance (Agriculture) Convention, 1933 (shelved)

37. Invalidity Insurance (Industry, etc.) Convention, 1933 (shelved)

38. Invalidity Insurance (Agriculture) Convention, 1933 (shelved)

39. Survivors' Insurance (Industry, etc.) Convention, 1933 (shelved)

40. Survivors' Insurance (Agriculture) Convention, 1933 (shelved)

41. Night Work (Women) Convention (Revised), 1934 (shelved)

42. Workmen's Compensation (Occupational Diseases) Convention (Revised), 1934

43. Sheet-Glass Works Convention, 1934 (shelved)

44. Unemployment Provision Convention, 1934 (shelved)

45. Underground Work (Women) Convention, 1935

46. Hours of Work (Coal Mines) Convention (Revised), 1935 (withdrawn by the ILC – decision of 15 June 2000)

47. Forty-Hour Week Convention, 1935

48. Maintenance of Migrants' Pension Rights Convention, 1935 (shelved)

49. Reduction of Hours of Work (Glass-Bottle Works) Convention, 1935 (shelved)

50. Recruiting of Indigenous Workers Convention, 1936 (shelved)

51. Reduction of Hours of Work (Public Works) Convention, 1936 (withdrawn by the ILC – decision of 15 June 2000)

52. Holidays with Pay Convention, 1936

53. Officers' Competency Certificates Convention, 1936

54. Holidays with Pay (Sea) Convention, 1936

55. Shipowners' Liability (Sick and Injured Seamen) Convention, 1936

56. Sickness Insurance (Sea) Convention, 1936

57. Hours of Work and Manning (Sea) Convention, 1936

58. Minimum Age (Sea) Convention (Revised), 1936

59. Minimum Age (Industry) Convention (Revised), 1937

60. Minimum Age (Non-Industrial Employment) Convention (Revised), 1937 (shelved)

61. Reduction of Hours of Work (Textiles) Convention, 1937 (withdrawn by the ILC – decision of 15 June 2000)

62. Safety Provisions (Building) Convention, 1937

63. Convention concerning Statistics of Wages and Hours of Work, 1938

64. Contracts of Employment (Indigenous Workers) Convention, 1939 (shelved)

65. Penal Sanctions (Indigenous Workers) Convention, 1939 (shelved)

66. Migration for Employment Convention, 1939 (withdrawn by the ILC – decision of 15 June 2000)

67. Hours of Work and Rest Periods (Road Transport) Convention, 1939 (shelved)

68. Food and Catering (Ships' Crews) Convention, 1946

69. Certification of Ships' Cooks Convention, 1946

70. Social Security (Seafarers) Convention, 1946

71. Seafarers' Pensions Convention, 1946

72. Paid Vacations (Seafarers) Convention, 1946

73. Medical Examination (Seafarers) Convention, 1946

74. Certification of Able Seamen Convention, 1946

75. Accommodation of Crews Convention, 1946

76. Wages, Hours of Work and Manning (Sea) Convention, 1946

77. Medical Examination of Young Persons (Industry) Convention, 1946

78. Medical Examination of Young Persons (Non-Industrial Occupations) Convention, 1946

79. Night Work of Young Persons (Non-Industrial Occupations) Convention, 1946

80. Final Articles Revision Convention, 1946

81. Labour Inspection Convention, 1947 Protocol of 1995 to the Labour Inspection Convention, 1947

82. Social Policy (Non-Metropolitan Territories) Convention, 1947

83. Labour Standards (Non-Metropolitan Territories) Convention, 1947

84. Right of Association (Non-Metropolitan Territories) Convention, 1947

85. Labour Inspectorates (Non-Metropolitan Territories) Convention, 1947

86. Contracts of Employment (Indigenous Workers) Convention, 1947 (shelved)

87. Freedom of Association and Protection of the Right to Organise Convention, 1948

88. Employment Service Convention, 1948

89. Night Work (Women) Convention (Revised), 1948 Protocol of 1990 to the Night Work (Women) Convention (Revised), 1948

90. Night Work of Young Persons (Industry) Convention (Revised), 1948

91. Paid Vacations (Seafarers) Convention (Revised), 1949 (shelved)

92. Accommodation of Crews Convention (Revised), 1949

93. Wages, Hours of Work and Manning (Sea) Convention (Revised), 1949

94. Labour Clauses (Public Contracts) Convention, 1949

95. Protection of Wages Convention, 1949

96. Fee-Charging Employment Agencies Convention (Revised), 1949

97. Migration for Employment Convention (Revised), 1949

98. Right to Organise and Collective Bargaining Convention, 1949

99. Minimum Wage Fixing Machinery (Agriculture) Convention, 1951

100. Equal Remuneration Convention, 1951

101. Holidays with Pay (Agriculture) Convention, 1952

102. Social Security (Minimum Standards) Convention, 1952

103. Maternity Protection Convention (Revised), 1952

104. Abolition of Penal Sanctions (Indigenous Workers) Convention, 1955 (shelved)

105. Abolition of Forced Labour Convention, 1957

106. Weekly Rest (Commerce and Offices) Convention, 1957

107. Indigenous and Tribal Populations Convention, 1957

108. Seafarers' Identity Documents Convention, 1958

109. Wages, Hours of Work and Manning (Sea) Convention (Revised), 1958

110. Plantations Convention, 1958 Protocol of 1982 to the Plantations Convention, 1958

111. Discrimination (Employment and Occupation) Convention, 1958

112. Minimum Age (Fishermen) Convention, 1959

113. Medical Examination (Fishermen) Convention, 1959

114. Fishermen's Articles of Agreement Convention, 1959

115. Radiation Protection Convention, 1960

116. Final Articles Revision Convention, 1961

117. Social Policy (Basic Aims and Standards) Convention, 1962

118. Equality of Treatment (Social Security) Convention, 1962

119. Guarding of Machinery Convention, 1963

120. Hygiene (Commerce and Offices) Convention, 1964

121. Employment Injury Benefits Convention, 1964 [Schedule I amended in 1980]

122. Employment Policy Convention, 1964

123. Minimum Age (Underground Work) Convention, 1965

124. Medical Examination of Young Persons (Underground Work) Convention, 1965

125. Fishermen's Competency Certificates Convention, 1966

126. Accommodation of Crews (Fishermen) Convention, 1966

127. Maximum Weight Convention, 1967

128. Invalidity, Old-Age and Survivors' Benefits Convention, 1967

129. Labour Inspection (Agriculture) Convention, 1969

130. Medical Care and Sickness Benefits Convention, 1969

131. Minimum Wage Fixing Convention, 1970

132. Holidays with Pay Convention (Revised), 1970

133. Accommodation of Crews (Supplementary Provisions) Convention, 1970

134. Prevention of Accidents (Seafarers) Convention, 1970

135. Workers' Representatives Convention, 1971

136. Benzene Convention, 1971

137. Dock Work Convention, 1973

138. Minimum Age Convention, 1973

139. Occupational Cancer Convention, 1974

140. Paid Educational Leave Convention, 1974

141. Rural Workers' Organisations Convention, 1975

142. Human Resources Development Convention, 1975

143. Migrant Workers (Supplementary Provisions) Convention, 1975

144. Tripartite Consultation (International Labour Standards) Convention, 1976

145. Continuity of Employment (Seafarers) Convention, 1976

146. Seafarers' Annual Leave with Pay Convention, 1976

147. Merchant Shipping (Minimum Standards) Convention, 1976 Protocol of 1996 to the Merchant Shipping (Minimum Standards) Convention, 1976

148. Working Environment (Air Pollution, Noise and Vibration) Convention, 1977

149. Nursing Personnel Convention, 1977

150. Labour Administration Convention, 1978

151. Labour Relations (Public Service) Convention, 1978

152. Occupational Safety and Health (Dock Work) Convention, 1979

153. Hours of Work and Rest Periods (Road Transport) Convention, 1979

154. Collective Bargaining Convention, 1981

155. Occupational Safety and Health Convention, 1981 Protocol of 2002 to the Occupational Safety and Health Convention, 1981

156. Workers with Family Responsibilities Convention, 1981

157. Maintenance of Social Security Rights Convention, 1982

158. Termination of Employment Convention, 1982

159. Vocational Rehabilitation and Employment (Disabled Persons) Convention, 1983

160. Labour Statistics Convention, 1985

161. Occupational Health Services Convention, 1985

162. Asbestos Convention, 1986

163. Seafarers' Welfare Convention, 1987

164. Health Protection and Medical Care (Seafarers) Convention, 1987

165. Social Security (Seafarers) Convention (Revised), 1987

166. Repatriation of Seafarers Convention (Revised), 1987

167. Safety and Health in Construction Convention, 1988

168. Employment Promotion and Protection against Unemployment Convention, 1988

169. Indigenous and Tribal Peoples Convention, 1989

170. Chemicals Convention, 1990

171. Night Work Convention, 1990

172. Working Conditions (Hotels and Restaurants) Convention, 1991

173. Protection of Workers' Claims (Employer's Insolvency) Convention, 1992

174. Prevention of Major Industrial Accidents Convention, 1993

175. Part-Time Work Convention, 1994

176. Safety and Health in Mines Convention, 1995

177. Home Work Convention, 1996

178. Labour Inspection (Seafarers) Convention, 1996

179. Recruitment and Placement of Seafarers Convention, 1996

180. Seafarers' Hours of Work and the Manning of Ships Convention, 1996

181. Private Employment Agencies Convention, 1997

182. Worst Forms of Child Labour Convention, 1999

183. Maternity Protection Convention, 2000

184. Safety and Health in Agriculture Convention, 2001

185. Seafarers' Identity Documents Convention (Revised), 2003

186. Maritime Labour Convention, 2006 [this Convention does not have a number]

187. Promotional Framework for Occupational Safety and Health Convention, 2006

188. Work in Fishing Convention, 2007

Bibliography

Agrawala, S., Ota, T., Ahmed, A.U., Smith, J. and van Aalst, M., Development and Climate Change in Bangladesh: Focus on Coastal Flooding and the Sundarbans, OECD, 2003

Borman, F.H. and Likens, G.E., The Nutrient Cycles of an Ecosystem, Scientific American, October 1970

Carroll, A.B. and Buchholz, A.K., Business and Society: Ethics and Stakeholder Management, South-Western Educational Publishing, Mason, 2000

Chapman, R., Culture Wars: An Encyclopaedia of Issues, Voices, and Viewpoints, Myron E. Sharpe, Armonk, New York, 2010

Chee, H.W. and Harris, R., Global Marketing Strategy, Financial Times/Prentice Hall, 1998

Chevron, Energy Supply & Demand, 2008, http://www.chevron.com/globalissues/energysupplydemand/

Crane, A. and Matten, D., Business Ethics, Oxford University Press, New York, 2003

Department for Economic and Social Affairs, Division for Sustainable Development, Trends in Sustainable Development: Agriculture, Rural Development, Land, Desertification and Drought, United Nations, Geneva, 2008

Dicken, P., Global Shift Transforming the World Economy, Paul Chapman Publishing, 1998

Dodds, F., Gardiner, R., Hales, D., Hemmati, M. and Lawrence, G., Post Johannesburg: The Future of the UN Commission on Sustainable Development, WHAT Governance Programme, Paper #9, November 2002

Doppelt, B., The Power of Sustainable Thinking: How to Create a Positive Future for the Climate, the Planet, Your Organization and Your Life, Earthscan Publications, London, 2008

GreenFacts Scientific Board, Scientific Facts on Biodiversity: A Global Outlook, 2008, http://www.greenfacts.org/en/global-biodiversity-outlook/index.htm

IPCC (Solomon, S., Qin, D., Manning, M., Chen, Z., Marquis, M., Averyt, K.B., Tignor, M. and Miller H.L. (ed.)), Summary for Policymakers. In: Climate Change 2007: The Physical Science Basis, Contribution of Working Group I to the Fourth Assessment Report of the Intergovernmental Panel on Climate Change, Cambridge University Press, Cambridge and New York, 2007

Kelkar, U. and Bhadwal, S., South Asian Regional Study on Climate Change Impacts and Adaptation: Implications for Human Development, Human Development Report 2007/2008: Fighting climate change: Human solidarity in a divided world, Human Development Report Office, United Nations Development Programme, 2007

Mbendi, World Oil and Gas, http://www.mbendi.com/indy/oilg/p0005.htm

New Scientist Environment and Reuters, Biofuel Production May Raise Price of Food, 9 May 2007, http://www.newscientist.com/article/dn11811-biofuel-production-may-raise-price-of-food--.html

OECD, OECD Annual Report 2009, Organisation for Economic Co-operation and Development, 2009

Pearce, D., Barbier, E. and Markandya, A., Sustainable Development: Economics and Environment in the Third World, Earthscan Publications, London, 1990

South Asia Region Sustainable Development Department, The World Bank South Asia: Shared Views on Development and Climate Change, The World Bank, Washington, 2009

Steffen, A., Worldchanging: A User's Guide for the 21st Century, Harry N. Abrams, Inc. New York, 2008

United Nations, Trends in Sustainable Development 2006-2007, New York 2006

United Nations, Millennium Development Goals Report 2008, United Nations, New York, 2008

UN-Energy, Energy in the United Nations: An overview of UN-Energy Activities, April 2006

UN-Energy, Sustainable Bioenergy: A Framework for Decision Makers, United Nations, 2007

UNEP (ed. Feenstra, J.F., Burton, I., Smith, J.B., and Tol, R.S.J., Handbook on Methods for Climate Change Impact Assessment and Adaptation Strategies, UNEP and the Institute for Environmental Studies, vrije Universiteit amsterdam, 1998

UNEP/Wuppertal Institute Collaborating Centre on Sustainable Consumption and Production, in collaboration with the Wuppertal Institute for Climate, Environment and Energy, A Background Paper prepared for the European Conference under the Marrakech Process on Sustainable Consumption and Production, Berlin, 13-14 December 2005

Vernadsky, V.I., The Biosphere: Complete Annotated Edition, Copernicus, an imprint of Springer-Veriag New York, Inc, 1997

Wessells, N.K. and Hopson, J.L., Biology, Random House, New York, 1988

World Commission on the Social Dimension of Globalisation, A Fair Globalisation: Creating Opportunities for All, International Labour Office, Geneva, 2004

References

(Endnotes)

1. Doppelt, B., *The Power of Sustainable Thinking: How to Create a Positive Future for the Climate, the Planet, Your Organization and Your Life*, Earthscan Publications, 2008

2. Press Association, *Tsunami Highlights Climate Change Risk*, http://www.guardian.co.uk/education/2004/dec/31/ highereducation.uk1, 31 December 2004

3. Pearce, D., Barbier, E. & Markandya, A., *Sustainable Development: Economics and Environment in the Third World*, Earthscan Publications, London, 1990

4. Vernadsky, V.I., *The Biosphere: Complete Annotated Edition*, Copernicus, an imprint of Springer-Veriag New York, Inc, 1997

5. Carroll, A.B. and Buchholz, A.K., *Business and Society: Ethics and Stakeholder Management*, South-Western Educational Publishing, 2000

6. Carroll, A.B. and Buchholz, A.K., *Business and Society: Ethics and Stakeholder Management*, South-Western Educational Publishing, 2000

7. United Nations, *Trends in Sustainable Development 2006-2007*, New York 2006

8.   Chapman, R., *Culture Wars: An Encyclopaedia of Issues, Voices, and Viewpoints*, Myron E. Sharpe, Armonk, New York, 2010

9.   World Commission on Environment and Development, *Our Common Future, Report of the World Commission on Environment and Development*, annex to General Assembly document A/42/427, 2 August 1987

10.   Annan, K., *Towards a Sustainable Future*, delivered at the American Museum of Natural History's annual 'Environmental Lecture' by Mrs Nane Annan, United Nations press release SG/SM/8239 ENV/DEV/637, 14 May 2002

11.   United Nations Department of Public Information, press release, 14 May 2002

12.   Cobb, L., http://en.wikipedia.org/wiki/World_population, 19 September 2008

13.   United Nations, Department for Economic and Social Affairs, Economic and Social Affairs, *World Population to 2300*, ST/ESA/SER.A/236, 2004

14.   U.S. Census Bureau, Population Division, *Historical Estimates of World Population*, http://www.census.gov/ipc/www/worldhis.html

15.   Population Division of the Department of Social and Economic Affairs of the United Nations Secretariat, *World Population Prospects: The 2008 Revision Population Database*, http://esa.un.org/unpp/

16.   Wilson, E.O., *The Diversity of Life*, Harvard University Press, 1992

17.   OECD

18.   UN-Energy, *The Energy Challenge for Achieving the Millennium Development Goals*, United Nations, 2005

19.   Local Government Declaration, www.iclei.org/Johannesburg/20002/wssd docs.html

20. Yale University's Centre for Environmental Law and Policy, Columbia University's Centre for International Earth Science Information Network, in collaboration with the World Economic Forum and the Joint Research Centre of the European Commission, *2005 Environmental Sustainability Index*, http://sedac.ciesin.columbia.edu/es/esi/downloads.html

21. Yale University's Centre for Environmental Law and Policy, Columbia University's Centre for International Earth Science Information Network, in collaboration with the World Economic Forum and the Joint Research Centre of the European Commission, *2005 Environmental Sustainability Index*, http://sedac.ciesin.columbia.edu/es/epi/downloads. html#summary

22. Kelkar, U. and Bhadwal, S., *South Asian Regional Study on Climate Change Impacts and Adaptation: Implications for Human Development, Human Development Report 2007/2008: Fighting climate change: Human solidarity in a divided world*, Human Development Report Office, United Nations Development Programme, 2007

23. Kelkar, U. and Bhadwal, S., *South Asian Regional Study on Climate Change Impacts and Adaptation: Implications for Human Development, Human Development Report 2007/2008: Fighting climate change: Human solidarity in a divided world*, Human Development Report Office, United Nations Development Programme, 2007

24. Klugman, J. et al., *Human Development Report 2010: Pathways to Human Development*, United Nations Development Programme, New York, 2010

25. Kelkar, U. and Bhadwal, S., *South Asian Regional Study on Climate Change Impacts and Adaptation: Implications for Human Development, Human Development Report 2007/2008: Fighting climate change: Human solidarity in a divided world*, Human Development Report Office, United Nations Development Programme, 2007

26. Meijer, S., Pusch, C. and Sinha R., *South Asia: Shared Views on*

Development and Climate Change, The World Bank (South Asia Region Sustainable Development Department), Washington DC, 2009

27. Countries included are Afghanistan, Bangladesh, Bhutan, India, Maldives, Pakistan, Nepal and Sri Lanka.

28. Agrawala, S., Ota, T., Ahmed, A.U., Smith, J. and van Aalst, M., *Development and Climate Change in Bangladesh: Focus on Coastal Flooding and the Sundarbans,* OECD, 2003

29. Dicken P., *Global Shift Transforming the World Economy,* Paul Chapman Publishing, 1998

30. Metro, 8 December 2006

31. The stages of textile production are fibre production; fibre processing, spinning; yarn preparation; fabric production; bleaching, dyeing and printing; and finishing. Each stages produces waste that requires proper management.

32. Just under half of all industrial locations in the country are located in the North Central region, of which 33% are textiles and finished garment factories. Of this, the Dhaka district accounts for almost half and Narayanganj almost a third.

33. Jraiw K., *Urban Road Transport in Asia's Developing Countries: Safety and Strategy,* Transportation Research Record No. 1846, 203, pp 19-25

34. The World Bank, http://siteresources.worldbank.org/ DATASTATISTICS/Resources/table3_13.pdf, 2007

35. The World Bank (Agriculture and Rural Development Sector Unit, South Asia Region), *India: Unlocking Opportunities for Forest-Dependent People in India, Main Report: Volume I* , Report No. 34481-IN, February 6, 2006

36. A research project undertaken by National Geographic and GlobeScan, http://environment.nationalgeographic.com/ environment/greendex/2008-survey/

37. Walsh, B., *The World's Most Polluted Places,* Time Magazine,

12 September 2007, http://www.time.com/time/specials/packages/completelist/0,29569,1661031,00.html

38. http://www.asiansr.com/

39. http://www.tata.com/ourcommitment/index.aspx?sectid=ei6stgDjpgA=

40. http://pib.nic.in/archieve/others/2010/may/d2010051103.pdf

41. Indian Brand Equity Foundation, *Corporate Responsibility / Human Resource*, June 2010, http://www.ibef.org/india/CSR.aspx

42. http://www.itcportal.com/default.aspx

43. http://timesfoundation.indiatimes.com/

44. http://www.infosys.com/sustainability/environment/Pages/index.aspx

45. Winkler, D. and Moser, C., *Growing the Jewel of the Ocean*, Monday Times, 3 September 2001

46. Winkler, D. and Moser, C., *Growing the Jewel of the Ocean*, Monday Times, 3 September 2001

47. United Nations Development Programme, *Human Development Report 2009*, http://hdr.undp.org/en/reports/global/hdr2009/

48. The World Bank (Sustainable and Development Unit, South Asia Region), *Pakistan: Promoting Rural Growth and Poverty Reduction*, Report No. 39303-PK, March 30, 2007

49. http://www.unep.org/ourplanet/imgversn/83/editoral.html

50. *Forest Sector Master Plan GOP 1992*, from *Environmental Profile of Pakistan*, 1998

51. The Nature of Pakistan

52. Government of Pakistan and IUCN/WWF, *Biodiversity Action Plan: Pakistan*, 1999

53. Green Living Association Pakistan, http://www. greenlivingasc.org/bio2.htm

54. Green Living Association Pakistan, http://www. greenlivingasc.org/bio2.htm

55. Green Living Association Pakistan, http://www. greenlivingasc.org/bio2.htm

56. Steffen, A., *Worldchanging: A User's Guide for the 21st Century*, Harry N. Abrams, Inc. New York, 2008

57. The University of Michigan, www.globalchange.umich.edu

58. *Overfishing: A Threat to Marine Biodiversity*, United Nations, 2006, http://www.un.org/events/tenstories/06/story. asp?storyID=800

59. *Millennium Ecosystem Assessment*, 2005, http://www.maweb. org/en/index.aspx

60. www.greenfacts.org

61. *Millennium Ecosystem Assessment*, 2005, http://www.maweb. org/en/index.aspx

62. *Millennium Ecosystem Assessment*, 2005, http://www.maweb. org/en/index.aspx

63. *Millennium Ecosystem Assessment*, 2005, http://www.maweb. org/en/index.aspx

64. *Millennium Ecosystem Assessment*, 2005, http://www.maweb. org/en/index.aspx

65. *Millennium Ecosystem Assessment*, 2005, http://www.maweb. org/en/index.aspx

66. *Millennium Ecosystem Assessment*, 2005, http://www.maweb. org/en/index.aspx

67. *Millennium Ecosystem Assessment*, 2005, http://www.maweb. org/en/index.aspx

68. US Energy Information Administration, www.eia.doe.gov

69. World Commission on the Social Dimension of Globalisation, *A Fair Globalisation: Creating Opportunities for All*, International Labour Office, Geneva, 2004

70. Halonen, T. and Mkapa, B.W., *Globalization Can and Must Change*, World of Work Magazine, No. 50, March 2004

71. Rio Declaration on Environment and Development, *Report of the United Nations Conference on the Human Environment, Stockholm*, United Nations publication, sales no. E.73.II.A.14 and corrigendum, 5-16 June 1972

72. www.mbendi.com

73. www.mbendi.com